JAZZ

THE GREAT AMERICAN ART

NEW HAVEN FREE PUBLIC LIBRARY
133 ELM STREET
NEW HAVEN, CT 06510

THE GREAT AMERICAN ART
by GENE SEYMOUR

FRANKLIN WATTS
A DIVISION OF GROLIER PUBLISHING

NEW YORK   LONDON   HONG KONG   SYDNEY
DANBURY, CONNECTICUT

This is going out to my father, who taught me how to listen.

G.S.

Grateful appreciation to Dan Morgenstern for his helpful comments and suggestions. Thanks are also given to New York Newsday for granting me the time and space to complete this work. And thanks, most of all, to Lorna Greenberg, my editor at Franklin Watts and Tom Cohn, a former Franklin Watts editor, who got me into this in the first place.

Frontis: Bill Evans, piano; Jimmy Cobb, drums; Paul Chambers, bass; Miles Davis, trumpet; John Coltrane, tenor sax

Photographs copyright ©: Frank Driggs Collection: pp. 2, 47, 54, 60, 72, 74, 116 (Joe Alper), 129 (Joe Alper), 137 (Joe Alper); Michael Ochs Archives: pp. 17, 18, 38, 93, 112 (BMI Photo Archives), 140; The Bettmann Archive: p. 20; New York Public Library, Picture Collection: p. 26; UPI/Bettmann: pp. 29, 99, 103, 109, 144, 149; William P. Gottlieb, Library of Congress, Ira and Lenore S. Gershwin Fund: pp. 41, 51, 66, 85, 90; Globe Photos: p. 63; Laura Friedman: p. 120.

Library of Congress Cataloging-in-Publication Data

Seymour, Gene.
    Jazz, the great American art / by Gene Seymour.
        p.   cm. — (The African-American experience)
    Includes bibliographical references, discography, and index.
    Summary: A history of jazz, from its roots in blues, ragtime, and swing to its various contemporary manifestations, discussing the major performers and the music's reflection of the experiences of African Americans.
        ISBN 0-531-11218-7
        1. Jazz—History and critcism—Juvenile literature.   2. Afro-American musicians—Juvenile literature.   [1. Jazz—History and criticism.   2. Afro-Americans—Music—History and criticism.]   I. Title.   II. Series.
ML3506.S44   1995
781.65'09—dc20   95-4693   CIP   MN   AC

CONTENTS

INTRODUCTION

All those people who had been slaves, they needed music more than ever now; it was like they were trying to find out in this music what they were supposed to do with this freedom: playing the music and listening to it—waiting for it to express what they needed to learn, once they had learned it wasn't just white people the music had to reach to, nor even to their own people, but straight out to life and to what a man does with his life when it finally is his.

—Sidney Bechet

ALL MY LIFE, I looked to African-American music for spiritual renewal and emotional release. Whatever form this music took (rhythm and blues, gospel, jazz), I believed it was as vital to my survival as food, water, and oxygen. The more I heard, the more I embraced the music's potential—and yearned for knowledge of its past.

By the time I'd gone to college in the early 1970s, that yearning had taken me to ragtime. This early twentieth-century syncopated music was undergoing a modest revival in those years due largely to the success of the 1973 Paul Newman–Robert Redford caper movie *The Sting*, with a score derived from the music of ragtime's most famous composer, Scott Joplin. The year before, I'd become enraptured with recordings of Joplin's piano rags by Joshua Rifkin, whose sensitive touch brought forth from this music a stirring balance of melancholy and resolve I recognized and loved in the works of both Monk and Mozart.

Not many of my fellow black students shared my sense of excitement. But they weren't put off by it. None, anyway, seemed as irritated with me as a white history major living in my dorm who, one evening, demanded to know how I could consider myself an Intellectually Aware Black Person and still enjoy ragtime. After all, he said, didn't I know that *Plessy v. Ferguson*, the notorious 1896 Supreme Court decision upholding racial segregation, came three years before Joplin wrote his first, and most popular piece, "Maple Leaf Rag"? Didn't I know that the years that followed—the first fifth of the twentieth century—were among the worst ever for black Americans?

Of course, I knew. That whole era, from the turn of the century to the end of World War I, was plagued by lynchings, race riots, viciously enforced segregation. It may well have been the peak of post–Civil War American apartheid. Knowing that ragtime was a big part of the soundtrack for those terrible years, how, the white student insisted, could I even *listen* to this stuff?

I remember sort of disconnecting from the whole discussion. It may have been the good intentions I heard stumbling blindly beneath his rancor. I may also have been feeling so secure with my own unshakable allegiance to black music that I thought it was unnecessary to get into an argument. What I was thinking, I suppose, ran along the lines of, *He has his opinion. I have my music. I have the better of the deal.*

Still, hindsight tells me I should have said something like this in reply: "Yes, those were terrible times. Possibly the worst ever. Which makes the music of Scott Joplin more miraculous. Maybe all *you* hear in Joplin's music is some kind of rinky-dinky background noise for the genteel brutality of an earlier time. What *I* hear is a black man's imagination staring down misery and dread. Each phrase, each note reminds me that embracing life makes up the first line of defense against despair, whether it's your own or belongs to those around you.

"How could I listen to this music? You're asking the wrong question. You should be asking me, how could I *not* listen to it?"

This book talks about just one product of black musical imagination; one which is vast, rich, and highly developed. It feeds—and, in turn, has been fed by—other types of black music and by music throughout the world. This music has been called America's greatest art form. And it shares many qualities with the land of its birth. It is vital, changeable, and, above all, complex.

The name given this music is jazz. And here, already, we run into trouble because no one really knows where the name came from. Some, nodding toward the music's deep ties to New Orleans and its French-Creole cultural traditions, speculate that the word sprang from the French verb *jasser,* loosely translated as "to chatter or have animated conversations among diverse people."[1]

In an earlier book, the poet Langston Hughes theorized: "Some say [the name] came from a player whose name was Jasper—Jas, for short. Some say the boy's name was Charles, but he wrote it abbreviated to Chas. . . . Others say that in New Orleans, in about 1900, there was a band called Razz's Band and that somehow the name of this band got changed to Jazz Band. . . ."[2]

We'll never know for sure. What we do know is that whites were responsible for attaching the name *jazz* to this African-rooted music and making it stick. The earliest-known use of the word was in a 1913 edition of a San Francisco newspaper: "The team which speeded into town this morning comes pretty close to representing the pick of the army. Its members have been trained on ragtime and jazz."[3]

The word would reappear over the next few years, published with various spellings: "jas," "jass," "jascz." The word was defined in some quarters as being synonymous with sexual intercourse, giving the music an aura that excited many listeners, scandalized others. Whatever the case, the name and the music were connected for the first time in 1917 with the debut of the Original Dixieland Jazz Band, an all-white group that became a sensation playing the kind of New Orleans music that African- and Creole-Americans like Buddy Bolden, Jelly Roll Morton, Sidney Bechet, and Joe "King" Oliver had been developing years before in relative obscurity. Still, these musicians would become famous along with the music. And they, too, would adopt *jazz* as a name for what they played.

Throughout much of its history, jazz found it hard to shake its low-life image from the minds of white listeners, however popular or sophisticated it became. The music's rough-hewn beginnings and its black lineage would combine to make many whites refuse to take it seriously at all. (The word *jazzy* is still used to describe an effort in the so-called higher arts that lacks depth or falls short of formal perfection.)

But to many other white listeners swept up by the music's vitality and power, it was precisely such status quo dismissal that endowed jazz—and, later, rock and roll—with rebellious overtones. African-American culture had its own "polite society" that disdained blues and jazz. But for the most part, black people viewed jazz as an occasion for collective celebration and as an affirmation of shared values. What many whites embraced as an outlet for rebellion, blacks viewed as a vehicle for self-expression and advancement.

Besides, African Americans' riskiest rebellion didn't unfold in ballrooms, clubs, and concert halls. Courtrooms, classrooms, polling places, and the streets themselves were the real stages for black challenges to the status quo. As opportunities increased for African Americans, so did collective pride in their heritage. Many African-American thinkers and musicians began to challenge the widespread use of "jazz" as a label, promoted and sanctioned by whites, to define a black-based art form with grand achievements and far-reaching influence. Duke Ellington, jazz's greatest composer, always brushed aside the jazz label as if it were a household pest.

Black musicians, as far back as the 1940s, rebelled against being perceived as little more than entertainers. This impulse would grow to all-out activism by the 1960s, as African-American musicians led the fight for greater appreciation of what the percussionist Max Roach prefers to call Black Classical Music.

Variations of this title have been put forth over the years—American Classical Music, African-American Improvisational Music. But the efforts by Ellington, Roach and others to diminish use of the word *jazz* to define the music have yet to take hold in the marketplace. And, likely, never will.

Still, America as a whole looks down on jazz less and less. Jazz courses at colleges and universities are increasing. By the 1990s, the country's major cultural institutions—Lincoln Center, the Smithsonian Institution, Carnegie Hall—had established programs for preserving and developing the music. As the music has gained such prestige, it has taken the name *jazz* along with it.

With such prestige, however, jazz risks losing its connection with a mass audience. Jazz hasn't been a major presence on the pop music charts for some time now. And even with the support of major cultural institutions, jazz still doesn't have the clout that symphony orchestras, opera and dance companies carry when struggling for government support or private endowments. Suspended between "serious" and "popular" culture, jazz needs all the friends it can get.

They're hard to find. Many people—black, white, old, young and in between—say they find this music (once as much a target for middle-class scorn as rock or rap) too obscure, too old-hat, too stodgy, too long-winded.

Some of you reading this book may be just as skeptical. You may believe, for instance, that jazz takes too long to "get to the point" compared with rock or rhythm-and-blues. A fan of rap and hip-hop once said he felt about jazz the way the Austrian emperor in the film *Amadeus* felt about Mozart's music. There are, he said, "just too many notes."

It depends. When listening, say, to Louis Armstrong or Miles Davis, you don't hear those two trumpeters playing a lot of notes. But the notes they *do* play are charged by the vivid, contrasting personalities of each man, whether it's Armstrong's exuberance or Davis's moodiness (sometimes vice versa). They are able to touch their audiences deeply, saying much with very little. All of which helps explain why they were so famous during their lifetime, and why their fame went beyond jazz itself.

Sonny Rollins, the great tenor saxophonist, once told me, "You can find just about anything in jazz. You can find humor. You can find sorrow. You can find passion. It's all there." He's right: you, as a listener, can open yourself to the intricate, unpredictable, never-the-same-way-twice interplay of melody, harmony, and rhythm that is jazz at its best.

In jazz—or whatever you want to call it—it's the journey more than the destination that counts.

one

Roots and Blues

ONCE THEY WERE put in chains and on ships bound for the Americas, they were no longer Yoruba, Ashanti, Dahomey, Ibo, or Fanti—except in their memories. They were black chattel.

These West African men and women had been torn from their clans, tribes, and families. They had been stripped of their dignity, their material possessions.

All they had was each other, the rituals and stories they kept to remind them they were alive—and their music.

How enslaved Africans retained and nurtured these fragments of their collective identity in America through 250 hard years of the Atlantic slave trade is one of the miracles of the human spirit.

After the slave trade ended, details about West African cultural connections with black America were sketchy and vague. But studies by anthropologists, musicologists, and historians searching for jazz's origins gradually, if inconclusively, fill in some of the blanks.

Many of these experts have found such aspects of jazz music as group improvisation, polyphony (a combination of two or more melodies), antiphony (call-and-response patterns in music) and syncopated rhythms in native African music. Some have made more specific connections. For instance, in the Yoruba language, writes composer Ortiz M. Walton, "the same word can have several meanings depending on the pitch of the word." What Walton describes as an "ingrained musical aesthetic" among Africans came about because of this sensitivity to pitch.[1] Such sensitivity made the *sound* a drum makes as important as the rhythm being played. This explains, in part, why drums were used by African tribes to communicate with each other.

In America, drums were so important to the Africans that some slaveholding states enacted antidrum laws. That didn't stop slaves from clapping their hands or stomping their feet instead. At times, such tapping, clapping, and stomping were used as a code system for escape plans.

African slaves also adapted many of their tribal rituals to white masters' demands that they convert to Christianity. From this melding of cultures came such phenomena as the "ring shout," An Americanized variation of a West African dance in which worshipers danced in a circle around a preacher in improvised, impassioned response to a song or sermon.

Spirituals were the most distinctive result of this mix of black musical tradition and white Protestant culture. These "sorrow songs" by slaves in worship services have endured for centuries. The emotion that went into the spirituals also emerged in the field hollers and work songs that slaves created spontaneously, to accompany the rhythms of their labor.

Before and after Emancipation, both spirituals and field hollers were vehicles for expressing not just sorrow, but defiance; not just resignation, but release. Whatever their meanings, these songs and chants came into being because black people needed an outlet for expressing musically *how it felt to be alive* at a given moment. All that we call art—whether it's music, painting, storytelling, poetry—comes from that same need.

One can't talk about jazz without talking about the blues, which evolved from a mix of spirituals and field hollers with European-based folk music and hymns. The blues, many argue, is *the* foundation for American popular music in the twentieth century. Almost certainly, the blues is the most crucial element in jazz's development as America's greatest home-grown art form. And jazz music, among other things, is just another way of playing or singing the blues.

Although blues music, as the historian Paul Oliver writes, "has provided a source of inspiration, even fundamental character to jazz,"[2] its history is separate from jazz's own. As with jazz, blues developed at the beginning of the twentieth century in different regions of the country and took on the personality of each region. Country blues, sometimes called "folk blues" or "Delta blues" because of its origins in the Mississippi River delta, is believed to be the earliest-known blues music that is still played, sung, and danced to in southern rural communities. Some of this music, along with its practitioners, migrated in the 1930s west to Texas or north to Memphis or Chicago.

The basic blues song has 12 measures and moves in 4/4 time. Its melodic-harmonic patterns are accented with tonal ornaments which came to be known as "blue notes." The lyrics of a basic blues song begin with a twice-repeated declaration followed by a new statement that completes the stanza the way a punch line completes a joke.

Here is an example:

It was early one Monday morning and I was on my way to school.

Yes, it was early in the morning and I was on my way to school.

That was the morning that I broke my mother's rule.

"The blues" has, for centuries, been employed as a term for melancholy or depression. Blues music, as critic Albert Murray writes, is something else entirely. "With all its so-called blue notes and overtones of sadness, blues music of its very nature and function is nothing if not a form of diversion."[3] No matter how dismal the content of a blues song, whether it deals with pain, loss, anxiety, dread, the song is an affirmation of life, not a lament.

Much of this attitude was established by the music's defining artists—the first, anyway, to have recorded the music. Foremost among these were Gertrude "Ma" Rainey (1886–1939), Blind Lemon Jefferson (1897–1930) and Huddie "Leadbelly" Ledbetter (1885–1949).

Jefferson and Ledbetter grew up in Texas. Jefferson, the younger man, whose mid-1920s recordings are still regarded as definitive country blues, exerted an influence on Ledbetter, who had first heard Jefferson in the bordellos of Dallas's red-light district. Ledbetter spent much of his life in and out of prison before achieving fame on the folk-music circuit in the 1940s. Though he is known more today for his folk dirge "Goodnight, Irene," Ledbetter's rhythmic playing on the twelve-string guitar influenced many blues, jazz, and rock guitarists.

Ma Rainey began making her reputation around the turn of the century in the vaudeville circuit, which she toured with her husband, Will "Pa" Rainey, and his Rabbit Foot Minstrels. Along with singers like Mamie Smith, the first blues singer to make a record (in 1920), Rainey defined the so-called classic blues style that followed the formal 12-bar structure and was performed with polished professionalism.

The greatest blues diva of all was Bessie Smith (1894–1937), who, to this day, is described in epic terms, both in the scope of her achievement and in her physical description. At five foot nine and about two hundred pounds, she was "a big, tall, handsome woman who exert-

Ma Rainey

Leadbelly

ed a majestic control over her audiences," writes Leonard Feather in the first volume of his *Encyclopedia of Jazz*.[4]

Born dirt-poor in Chattanooga, Tennessee, Smith worked in honky-tonks, carnivals, and tent shows for several years before she was taken to New York in 1923 to record "Downhearted Blues." Several recordings followed and within a year, Smith had sold two million records. Between 1923 and 1933, she recorded dozens of blues songs with some of jazz's greatest artists. Her galvanizing presence in a 1929 film short suggests that she could have been as big a star in the movies as on records. But a period of decline, brought on partly by alcoholism, came with the new decade. In 1937, she died in an automobile accident.

Smith's 1925 performance of "St. Louis Blues," with young Louis Armstrong accompanying her on cornet, is regarded by historians as perhaps the greatest blues recording of its time. The piece was written in 1914 by W. C. Handy (1873–1958), a bandleader, cornetist, and songwriter, who, throughout his long life, was called the "Father of the Blues." Born in Florence, Alabama, Handy was at various times a vagabond glee-club singer, music teacher, concert bandmaster, and song publisher.

Handy didn't invent the blues. But he synthesized many of the raw elements of blues music and incorporated them into written works like "Beale Street Blues," "Joe Turner's Blues," and "Memphis Blues" that set the standard for jazz compositions that followed. Handy, wrote jazz historian Marshall Stearns,

> *proved that jazz could make money. Or perhaps it would be more accurate to say that Handy showed how something of this jazz music could be written down and sold. . . . And when tunes even remotely derived from jazz make a lot of money, jazz itself commands immediate attention. The growth and spread of jazz is speeded up. . . . Jazz gets a chance to sell itself.*[5]

Bessie Smith

Robert Johnson (1911–1938) never achieved, in his brief lifetime, Handy's esteem or Bessie Smith's fame. Yet his influence on American music is just as hard to ignore. Born in Hazelhurst, Mississippi, Johnson began playing blues guitar in his twenties, inspired by the example of such masters of Delta blues as Charlie Patton and Son House.

These men worked in a blues style that, while following the same basic harmonic and lyrical pattern of "classic blues," was rougher, tougher, and far less formalized than the music written by Handy and performed by Smith. Those who performed Delta blues were nomads, traveling all over the South, and becoming folk legends. Johnson's legend would endure the longest.

Johnson's reputation rests on a mere twenty-nine songs he recorded in two sessions—one that spread over four days in November 1936, in a San Antonio hotel room, the other, over two days in June 1937. On the basis of these recordings, eleven of which were released in his lifetime, Johnson seemed poised for discovery well beyond the Delta. But he died at twenty-eight from drinking poisoned whiskey.

The beat and harmonic pattern of Johnson's songs are basically similar to those of other Mississippi Delta blues. So are the subjects—travail, desire, loneliness, and the Devil, whose looming presence dogged the dreams of blues musicians fearing that their Saturday-night performances might offend the Good Lord and His Sunday-morning supplicants.

It is what Johnson does with these elements that startles even through the hiss and static of primitive recordings. At times, his chords come at you with such speed and intensity that you can't believe he's playing alone. Lyrics like the opening of "Stones in My Passway" also show that Johnson had a natural gift for stark, strange poetry:

I got stones in my passway and my road seems dark
   at night.

I got stones in my passway and my road seems dark
   at night.
I have pains in my heart. They have taken my ap-
   petite.

In the years after Johnson's death, his songs influenced blues artists like Muddy Waters, John Lee Hooker, Sonny Boy Williamson, and Howling Wolf. Johnson was also claimed as an inspiration to rock-and-roll stars like the Rolling Stones, Eric Clapton, Prince, and Bob Dylan. Johnson's direct influence on jazz music is more difficult to define. But he belongs here because he represents the supreme example of an African-American artist who took hold of his craft, brought to it the full measure of his personality and imagination, and created inventions so singular that they sound fresh even today. The history of jazz is propelled by many such artists.

two

OF RAGGY RHYTHMS AND GREAT STRIDES

OF ALL THE MYTHS about jazz, the one that may be hardest to kill goes like this: Jazz music was born in New Orleans and made its way up the mighty Mississippi River to Chicago and then found its way to New York, where it began its conquest of the world.

New Orleans does have an important place in jazz's history. But the music's real origins are a jumble of cross-fertilized ideas and traditions, springing from various regions all over the country.

Another myth is that the real birthplace of jazz is farther up the Mississippi from New Orleans. St. Louis, Missouri, which, among other things, was the subject of W. C. Handy's best-known blues tune, was the center of the ragtime era in American popular music.

Ragtime was the first African-American music to achieve popularity among whites and blacks alike. It was a blend of African and European musical elements, carrying echoes of the ring dance, cakewalk, reel, jig, polka, and other dance music.

A ragtime piece, when played (as it usually is) by a solo piano, involves the use of the left hand to set down the vertical beat (as in the OOM-pah, OOM-pah rhythm of a band) while the right hand either augments the rhythm or plays the melodic figures. "The left hand," the saying went, "is the drummer while the right hand is the dreamer."

Syncopated music like this was spreading through the traveling minstrel shows bringing cakewalk dancing and songs to vaudeville stages throughout the United States in the late nineteenth and early twentieth centuries. (The cakewalk, a combination of a prance and a promenade, was derived from harvest celebrations on southern plantations where slaves competed for prizes. Often a cake was first prize.)

It was in the Midwest, specifically St. Louis and more specifically the nearby town of Sedalia, Missouri, where the ragtime music now regarded as classic took root and flourished. Tom Turpin (1873–1922), Arthur Marshall (1881–1956), and Louis Chauvin (1883–1908) were three notable black ragtime pianist-composers whose home base was the St. Louis-Sedalia area. In 1897, Turpin's "Harlem Rag" became the first published rag by a black composer. Chauvin, some historians believe, was the first notable ragtime pianist. James Scott (1886–1938) made a considerable reputation as a composer with such works as "Evergreen Rag" (1915) and "Kansas City Rag" (1907). Joseph F. Lamb (1887–1960), although white and from Montclair, New Jersey, wrote two of the authentic classics of the ragtime era, "Ethiopia Rag" (1909) and "Champagne Rag" (1910).

None of these men would harvest the fame or suffer the heartbreak of Scott Joplin (1868–1917), the greatest ragtime composer of all. Born in Texarkana, Texas, Joplin, who grew up in a family of musicians, became fascinated with the piano, at age eight. His father, an ex-slave who played violin, pieced together money to buy him an old grand piano, and by eleven, the younger Joplin was improvising well enough to attract the attention of an elderly German music teacher who took him as a pupil.

Joplin left home in his early teens to seek his fortune through music. He ended up in the St. Louis-Sedalia area in the mid-1880s and began playing in honky-tonks and on concert stages. In 1893, he went to the World's Columbian Exposition in Chicago, where he and many other musicians played some of the ragtime music that was brewing back in Missouri. He settled in Sedalia to play and write the rags that would make him famous.

His breakthrough came in 1899 with the publication of "Maple Leaf Rag," which effectively made him "king of ragtime." In the following years, Joplin wrote more than fifty piano pieces, a ballet showcasing black social dances, and two operas. These works demonstrated the range of Joplin's ambition, which may have been fulfilled only in piano rags. He stretched the genre's harmonic and thematic possibilities in "Euphonic Sounds" (1909), "Solace—A Mexican Serenade" (1909), "Gladiolus Rag" (1907), and "Magnetic Rag" (1914).

Joplin's sheet music often included the instruction: "Do not play this piece fast. It is never right to play 'Ragtime' fast." And indeed, when this dictum is followed by contemporary interpreters of Joplin's work, the wistful lyricism and almost haunting melancholy of his work are brought out. (A few surviving piano rolls made from Joplin's own playing offer testimony to his piano skills, which, legend has it, were remarkable.)

But Joplin's life, for all its achievement, was marred by tragedy. His first marriage foundered after the death of an infant son. Not long afterward, in 1907, he moved to New York. He wrote some of his more complex and less successful rags during this period. He also started writing

Scott Joplin

Treemonisha (1911), an ambitious three-act opera about a young black child, found beneath a tree, who grows up to battle superstition and ignorance to become a leader of her people.

The opera was performed once, in 1915, without scenery or orchestra, in front of a predominantly black middle-class audience whose members apparently resented the opera's references to a past they had left behind. The failure of the enterprise, which Joplin had financed, produced, and supervised himself, took an emotional and physical toll on the composer. In 1916, he was committed to the Manhattan State Hospital on Ward's Island, suffering from "dementia paralytica cerebral." As with many American artists, Joplin struggled to find a balance between his need for creative fulfillment and the demands of the marketplace. He died in April 1917, five days before the United States entered World War I. Both events, in effect, marked the end of the age of ragtime.

It was in the 1970s, a time of growing acknowledgment of black culture, that Joplin was given the artistic respectability that eluded him for much of his life. His opera *Treemonisha* was given a handsomely mounted revival in 1975 by the Houston Grand Opera. And his rag "The Entertainer" was a popular hit two years before, as the theme from the movie *The Sting*. In fact, the entire score of that film was based on Joplin tunes like "The Ragtime Dance" and "Solace."

Toward the end of Joplin's life, the ragtime music he helped popularize was curving and bending in various new shapes throughout the United States. Clubs in New York's Harlem section were staging areas for a variant of ragtime that would become known as "stride piano," probably because its rhythms dare you to move in long, vigorous steps.

The master of this style was James P. Johnson (1894–1955), a New Jersey–born pianist who brought his thorough classical training to Harlem, where he encountered other piano-playing prodigies like Luckey Roberts (1895–1965) and Eubie Blake (1883–1983).

These pianists —"ticklers," as Johnson, in an interview many years later, says they were called[1]—engaged in duels as keen as any one-on-one basketball contest. They competed in dress, manner, and approaches to the keyboard, whether playing in clubs or at rent parties in Harlem apartments.

One tune that these pianists especially strived to perfect was Johnson's "Carolina Shout," which was first issued on piano roll in 1918. Johnson's piece was built like a rag, but its rhythmic drive shifted and bent in a manner that dazzled its listeners, especially young pianists like Duke Ellington, who learned to play the piece by slowing down the piano roll so he could see where the keys went up and down.

Other young pianists following "James P.'s" lead in stride piano included Willie "The Lion" Smith (1897–1973) and Thomas "Fats" Waller (1904–1943). Waller is best remembered as a comic performer with broad facial expressions and a cagey approach to singing. He was also a resourceful pianist. Like Blake, who wrote such popular chestnuts as "I'm Just Wild about Harry," and Johnson, best known throughout his life as the writer of the Jazz Age anthem "The Charleston," Waller was a gifted composer. His "Honeysuckle Rose" and "Ain't Misbehavin'" became standards in the jazz repertoire.

Waller's appearances in such movies as the musical *Stormy Weather* made him widely known. Greater popularity could have been his if he hadn't died suddenly in December 1943 while riding a transcontinental train from Los Angeles to New York City.

Waller's fame eclipsed that of his mentor, James P. Johnson, who shared with *his* mentor, Joplin, grand aspirations for ragtime music. Johnson wrote many symphonies,

Fats Waller

suites, concertos, ballets, and musical comedies, including *Sugar Hill*, which ran briefly in 1948. He was incapacitated by a stroke in 1951 and died four years later. By then, Ellington, Count Basie, Art Tatum, and Thelonious Monk all claimed the "father of stride piano" as a shared influence for their distinctive styles.

three

CRESCENT CITY

BY NOW, we're so used to having radios and stereos around that it's hard to imagine a time when music's main routes to mass recognition were through the parlor piano or the outdoor band concert. But that's how American songs reached the public before the twentieth century.

Band music, especially, offered a sort of nineteenth-century equivalent to today's Hot 100. Parades, picnics, pageants, and public celebrations of all kinds engaged all Americans, even those who were not free Americans.

As early as the mid-1850s, there were black bands throughout the South made up of freed slaves and house slaves. Field slaves had no opportunity to be part of such bands until after the Civil War. When these newly emancipated slaves were able to play European instruments, West African rhythmic and harmonic influences began seeping into European-inspired martial music.

Nowhere was this interaction as dramatic as in New Orleans. Befitting its French origins, this sultry port city was especially drawn to the Napoleonic aura of the military march. (It was, in fact, at the time of Napoleon—the early 1800s—that the vogue for military band music was at its worldwide peak.)[1]

In the late nineteenth century, black bands had become a vital part of New Orleans cultural life. These bands were supported by a host of black clubs, lodges, orders and secret societies. When a member of a club died, the band led the funeral march, maybe several bands, since, as banjoist Danny Barker recalled, "a member was probably active in three or four organizations."[2]

The musicians would play a slow dirge on the way to the grave. After the burial, the band would march away from the cemetery with the drums setting a brisker, brighter tempo than before. A block or two away from the cemetery, all stops were pulled and a joyous release of music and dance would follow. "In New Orleans, they believed truly to stick right close to the Scripture," Jelly Roll Morton told folklorist Alan Lomax. "That means *rejoice at the death and cry at the birth.*"[3]

But then, New Orleans always offered fertile ground for black musical expression. With its strong Catholic heritage and a rich mix of French and Spanish influences, the region provided a hospitable environment for many of the *voudon* (hoodoo, as it was known in the continental United States; voodoo in the Caribbean) rituals that members of some African tribes retained in New World captivity.

More important to the future of American music, New Orleans also offered a haven from white slaveholders' ban on drumming. The city set aside an empty lot called Place Congo or Congo Square where slaves were permitted to sing, dance, and act out sacred rituals with makeshift drums and primitive instruments like thumb pianos, four-string banjos, and gourds filled with pebbles.[4]

With all this as background, there's little wonder that New Orleans is so important in the history of jazz. Some historians believe such importance is overstated because blues, ragtime, and band music were developing in other regions at the same time. But no one can deny preeminence to a city which has given to the world such artists as Jelly Roll Morton, Sidney Bechet, Joe "King" Oliver, and most important of all, Louis Armstrong.

Before these, there was the legendary figure of Charles "Buddy" Bolden. The few established facts about Bolden are these: He was born in New Orleans in 1877, worked as a plasterer, played cornet, and led many bands. He was the first to receive the nickname "King," in tribute to his musical ability. At age twenty-nine, he suffered a nervous breakdown in the middle of a parade and was committed to the Angola State Hospital, where he died in 1931.

Bolden's performances have been described by so many prominent witnesses—Morton, Bechet, Armstrong among them—that his importance in jazz history is accepted even without a recording. (Anyone who found one, just one, would be regarded as the Indiana Jones of jazz archives. No one has. Likely, no one will.)

Bolden was "the most powerful trumpet in history," according to Morton, who often overstated things (but mostly about himself). "Any time it was a quiet night at Lincoln Park because maybe the affair hadn't been so well publicized, Buddy Bolden would publicize it. He'd turn his big trumpet around toward the city and blow his blues, calling his children home as he used to say."[5]

Armstrong, who was six years old when Bolden was committed, remembered hearing Bolden "blow[ing] awful hard. . . . All in all, I think he blew too hard. I will even go so far as to say he did not blow correctly. In any case he finally went crazy. You can figure that out for yourself."[6]

Most anecdotes about Bolden speak more of his force than his technique. Some say he was better with blues songs like "Careless Love" than with rag tunes of the time.

One thing they agree on: In just about every "carving" contest (a musical duel between instrumentalists of different bands), Bolden prevailed. (Later these would be called "cutting contests," with bands and individual musicians pitted against each other.) They also agree that he drank too much, lived too fast, flared out too quickly.

Bolden's musical links to jazz are inconclusive. But from all the stories, one gets an image of a "King" Bolden who looks a lot like the self-destructive mythic heroes of American music—Charlie Parker, Hank Williams, Billie Holiday, Elvis Presley—who would haunt the dream life of the twentieth century.

The end of the nineteenth century marked the beginning of an especially brutal time for African Americans. After Reconstruction ended in 1876 and federal troops were withdrawn from the South, racial segregation spread through the region with a vengeance. By the 1890s, segregation had become public law in many parts of the South; even in New Orleans, where the complex issue of color was intertwined with equally complex matters of social standing.

For many years, Canal Street served as the dividing line between the elegant, upper-class part of New Orleans to the east (downtown) and the rougher-hewn, more Americanized New Orleans to the west (uptown). The French side was populated with whites, black servants, and Creoles of color. The latter were mixed-race people who maintained elevated social and cultural standards regardless of whether they were accepted by the larger white society. Poor, less formally educated ex-slaves made up the population base of those living west of Canal.

Then in 1894, New Orleans adopted a restrictive racial code forcing the Creoles of color to live "uptown" with the rest of the city's blacks. Cultures clashed. Creole musicians were classically trained and prided themselves on a soft, nuanced approach to their instruments. The darker-skinned uptown musicians, meanwhile, played hard and more by ear than by sight-reading. We can only guess how the refined Creole sensibility mixed with the compulsive inventiveness of African-American musicians in this active New Orleans musical scene.

Probably the greatest leveling force for light- and dark-skinned musicians was the 1897 city ordinance restricting all New Orleans prostitutes to a thirty-eight-block area called Storyville. Within this "red-light" district, musicians of all colors found work as solo pianists or as members of small combos and brass bands. The intense musical activity spilled over into the cabarets, dance halls, river-boats, hotels, and cafes throughout the city.

The world wouldn't know much about the music that came into being in Crescent City until 1917, when the Original Dixieland Jazz Band, an ensemble of white New Orleans musicians, traveled to New York to make the first recordings of the polyphonic, syncopated sound that, from that point on, would be known as jazz.

Today, the Dixieland band isn't remembered much for its music. And the claims of its leader, Nick La Rocca, to be the founder of jazz, would be discredited in later years by musicians and archivists. But the impact of the band's recordings was undeniable. Like W. C. Handy's sheet music, the Dixieland Jazz Band's records proved that jazz could make lots of money. Both the success and the energy of these sounds would inspire musicians all over the country, white and black, to play them and, whenever possible, improve on them.

In the same significant year of the Dixieland record-ings, Scott Joplin died, America entered World War I, and Storyville, crucible for the New Orleans sound, was closed down by the U.S. Navy, forcing many of the city's finest players to seek work in other cities, like Chicago and New York, and even as far away as California, or Paris.

The world was changing. And many believed jazz was causing those changes as much as it was reflecting them.

Nick La Rocca wasn't the only one to make the dubious claim to have "founded" jazz. To the end of his crowded and colorful life, Ferdinand Morton (1890–1941), known best by his nickname, "Jelly Roll," told anyone who asked that he was the "inventor of jazz."

Morton's boast was typical of a gifted man with an inflated and, hence, fragile ego. Jazz was too complex in its development for any one person to be called its "inventor." Still, the contributions made to jazz by this dashing Creole musical prodigy, pool hustler, whorehouse pianist, vagabond showman, and composer came close to matching the grand claims he made for himself.

According to the testimony of such witnesses as trumpeter Bunk Johnson, Morton was barely into his teens when he was writing rags and playing piano professionally throughout New Orleans. His only peer as a pianist in those years was Tony Jackson, who was envied by Morton for his skill at playing both the blues and the classics.

Morton says he wrote his first piece, "New Orleans Rag," in 1902, when, if baptismal records are to be believed, he was twelve years old! It was also around this time, he says, that he started to develop his theories about jazz music: "It's to be played sweet soft, plenty rhythm, plenty swing," he told his biographer, Alan Lomax, in 1938. "When you have your plenty rhythm with your plenty swing, it becomes beautiful. . . . If a glass of water is full, you can't fill it any more, but if you have half a glass, you have the opportunity to put more water in it. Jazz music is based on the same principle."[7]

Jazz music, Morton said, should "always have a melody going some kind of way against a background of perfect harmony with plenty of riffs." (A riff is a musical phrase that is repeated behind a soloist or a theme.) Morton also claims to have pioneered the proper deployment of breaks, which he describes as "musical surprises."[8]

Some of Morton's best-known works, like "King Porter

Stomp" and "Jelly Roll Blues," were written at about the time he said he was making these innovations. These tunes were built like ragtime pieces. But when Morton later recorded them on solo piano or with a small band, they curved, jumped, and shook with bluesy energy and virtuoso inventiveness. Whether this was how they were originally performed is not known.

It was in 1908, Morton says, that he left New Orleans for good. He traveled far and wide—to Texas, Chicago, St. Louis, New York (where James P. Johnson remembered seeing him perform in 1911), Memphis, Mexico, California and in the early 1920s back to Chicago, where he made his first recordings. His own reminiscences, combined with those of people he'd met along the way, suggest an epic journey through several jobs, several lives. By the time he got to Chicago, he was sporting a diamond in his upper teeth.

The recordings he made between 1926 and 1930 were to bring him the fame and glory he felt were his due as jazz's "inventor." Plenty of people, then and now, thought he was more flash than substance. One prominent skeptic was Duke Ellington, who, in those years, was developing jazz composition well beyond Morton's own designs. Ellington believed Morton's only genius was for self-promotion.

And yet, listening now to the late-1920s recordings of pieces like "The Pearls," "Jungle Blues," "Wolverine Blues," "Kansas City Stomps," "Mournful Serenade," "Doctor Jazz," "Dead Man's Blues," one can't help feeling that Morton and his Red Hot Peppers—including trombonist Edward "Kid" Ory, banjo player Johnny St. Cyr, and clarinetist Omer Simeon—were establishing principles for all jazz ensemble playing that followed.

Morton filled his "half-empty glass" of music with all manner of rhythmic and melodic shifts, spirited riffs, deftly timed breaks. Yet the basic arrangements remain tightly con-

Jelly Roll Morton and the Red Hot Peppers:
Andrew Hilaire, drums; Kid Ory, trombone;
George Mitchell, cornet; Johnny Lindsey, bass;
Jelly Roll Morton, piano; Johnny St. Cyr, banjo;
Omer Simeon, clarinet

trolled. Every bandleader since, Ellington included, has followed this imperative, improving and amplifying it at every step taken along the path that Morton cleared—if, that is, he did clear the path. But whether Morton was jazz's "inventor" doesn't make his recordings any less valuable.

Other New Orleans musicians would seek their fortunes beyond the Crescent City as Storyville drifted into legend. Among the first to leave was the cornetist Freddie Keppard (1889–1933), whose reputation in New Orleans was such that he was considered the heir to the "throne" left vacant after "King" Buddy Bolden's breakdown in 1907. Keppard, along with Bill Johnson's Original Creole Band, left the city in 1912, or maybe 1913.

Stories also differ on where Keppard and his band went. Some place them in Los Angeles in 1914. Others have them in Chicago the same year. As early as 1915, the band was seen on vaudeville stages in New York City before it broke up in 1918 and Keppard settled in Chicago.

In its heyday, Keppard's band was so popular that it had a chance to make the first jazz record before the Original Dixieland Jazz Band's breakthrough. It didn't happen. Why? Again, stories differ. One says that Keppard didn't want his coveted style copied by other musicians. (Louis Armstrong recalls that whenever Keppard played in a street parade he would cover his fingers with a handkerchief "so that the other cornet players wouldn't catch his stuff.")[9] Still another story insists that Keppard wanted more money than the record company was willing to pay. He is said to have asked for as much as the opera star Enrico Caruso was getting. Whichever story is true, Keppard missed out on a chance for fame. By the time he recorded, in the mid-1920s, he was past his prime.

Among the many musicians who played with Keppard both in and out of New Orleans was Sidney Bechet (1897–1959), a Creole clarinetist who sat in with Keppard's band at age eight. Seven years later, he was introduced to the famous Eagle band by trumpeter Bunk Johnson (whose own renown would grow much later, in the 1940s, in the revival of interest in New Orleans music).

Beginning in 1914, Bechet toured Texas and other southern states with pianist-composer Clarence Williams. Bechet returned to New Orleans in 1916 to play with King Oliver's Olympia Band. In 1917, he moved to Chicago, where he played with Tony Jackson, Keppard, and Oliver. Two years later, he moved to New York City.

In 1919, Will Marion Cook's Southern Syncopated Orchestra was formed to embark on a European tour with Bechet. While overseas, the group came to the attention of the Swiss classical conductor Ernest Ansermet, who wrote that Bechet's "own way" of playing "is perhaps the highway the world will swing along tomorrow."[10]

Although he would continue to record and perform in America, off and on, for the rest of his life, Bechet would enjoy greater renown in Europe, especially in France, where he was a national institution. Yet his sweet style on clarinet and, most especially, on soprano saxophone would leave a lasting memorial.

The New Orleans musician-bandleader who had the greatest impact on jazz music to come was Joseph "King" Oliver (1885–1938). After Bolden and Keppard, Oliver was considered Crescent City's premier cornetist (hence the regal nickname).

Blinded in one eye in a boyhood accident, Oliver started out on the trombone then switched to cornet. He made his reputation in several brass bands, even leading one of his own, before heading to Chicago in 1918. Within four years, Oliver would lead the most polished, versatile and creative ensemble in all of jazz music. The addition of Louis Armstrong, an Oliver disciple from New Orleans days, to Oliver's Creole Jazz Band in 1922 was the capstone for a formidable group.

Together this band would, in 1923, make the first jazz recordings by an all-black group. Those records—

Sidney Bechet

"Dippermouth Blues," "Tears," "Canal Street Blues," "Sweet Lovin' Man," and "Chimes Blues" among them—have the same hard-driving rhythms and dazzling musicianship as Morton's recordings would a couple of years later. Yet Oliver and his band recorded when this music was still fresh and new to its listeners, many of whom had never heard the kinds of things Oliver was doing with a horn. Using mutes, cups, bottles, and other gadgets, Oliver gave an almost human voice to jazz instrumental performance.

There was no question, then or later, that the polyphonic sound of New Orleans ensemble jazz had reached a peak with this group, many of whose members would break away within a year to make some more history on their own. Oliver found replacements, but it was never the same.

Worse still, physical problems began to plague the King. Unlike Bolden and Keppard, Oliver didn't drink and hence avoided their fate. But Oliver did have a wicked sweet tooth. The word *wicked* is appropriate, given what Oliver's sugar habit would do to his teeth and gums—and the effect his dental problems would have on his playing. Oliver would cease recording after 1931. He continued to lead bands until 1936, when he settled down in Savannah, Georgia. He lived there in relative obscurity and poverty until his death seven years later.

To the end of his own life, Louis Armstrong would never miss a chance to praise his old mentor. "No one had the fire and the endurance Joe had. No one in jazz created as much music as he has. Almost everything important in music came from him."[11]

Jelly Roll Morton's life in Depression era America was, for a while, no less dismal than Oliver's. By the time Oliver died, Morton was running a small Washington, D.C., nightclub, tinkling away the evenings on a piano in obscurity until folklorist Alan Lomax approached him to record his life story, along with some piano solos, for the Library of Congress. In 1939, Morton returned to New York for recording sessions with, among others, Sidney Bechet. "Didn't He Ramble," "I Thought I Heard Buddy Bolden Say," and other tunes from Storyville's heyday were given surprisingly robust readings by Morton and company. These recordings would be his epitaph. He died in California in 1941.

You may have to push your senses back in time a little to figure out what got people so excited about this music that they named the whole 1920s "The Jazz Age" after it.

And yet once you've listened to jazz in any other era, you can come back to the music of Oliver, Morton, and the best of their peers to discover how original they were. The music they made will remind you of nothing you've ever heard—except everything that came later.

four

Pops

THE BRICK HOUSE, a honky-tonk bar in a small town not far from New Orleans, was a place where men who worked along the Mississippi River blew off steam. It didn't sound like a comfortable place to play one's horn for money. But gigs were hard to come by after Storyville was shut down in 1917. So a cornet player named Louis Armstrong (1901–1971) took a job playing every Saturday night at the Brick House.

Years later, Armstrong would describe this honky-tonk as "one of the toughest joints I ever played in. . . . Guys would drink and fight one another like circle saws. Bottles would come flying over the bandstand like crazy and there was lots of plain common shooting and cutting. But somehow all that jive didn't faze me at all, I was so happy to have some place to blow my horn."[1]

Bottles, bullets, and bloodshed and, through it all, Louis Armstrong is tending to his music, his calling. This vignette tells a great deal about the grace, heroism, and determination of this extraordinary man.

Armstrong was born poor. He never went past the third grade. Yet his rich imagination and dynamic personality made him one of the twentieth century's most beloved and important artists. In jazz, in entertainment, in much else, Louis Armstrong—also known as "Pops," "Dippermouth," "Satchel Mouth," or just plain "Satch"—changed everything that came before him and affected everything that followed.

Yet being one of the world's most famous men didn't protect Armstrong from bigotry and condescension from whites, along with criticism and contempt from blacks who believed he didn't oppose racism with enough vigor. He was threatened with death by underworld gangsters and put under surveillance by the FBI. Critics accused him, before and after his death, of selling out his artistry for "mere entertainment." Armstrong felt the sting of these assaults. But, as with the bottles and bullets at Brick Alley, he didn't let such "jive" get in the way of his music.

The man who would someday dine with royalty and entertain presidents, grew up in the poorest, roughest neighborhood in New Orleans, an area so crime-ridden it was known as "the Battlefield." Armstrong's father, an illiterate turpentine-factory worker, left his family when Louis was still a child. The boy was raised by his grandmother and his mother, Mayann, both of whom encouraged his keen survival instincts and instilled values of common decency. But neither of these kept him from being arrested when he was thirteen for shooting a pistol, loaded with blanks, outdoors during a Fourth of July celebration. He was sent to the Colored Waifs' Home, a local reformatory, where he received his first music lessons—and his first cornet. He was released after one year and took various menial jobs, including delivering coal with a mule and a wheelbarrow.

Although word spread through Crescent City about the young boy with the big-sounding horn, Armstrong didn't catch a real break until Joe Oliver took him under his wing, tutoring and encouraging him. Shortly after World War I ended in 1918, Oliver recommended his protégé as his replacement in trombonist Kid Ory's band.

That job led to many others. Perhaps Armstrong's most significant engagement in the years immediately after the war was with pianist Fate Marable, who led bands that performed aboard riverboats traveling up and down the Mississippi River. As Gary Giddins writes, "When people talk about jazz traveling up the river, they are paying tribute to Marable whether they know it or not."[2] At various stops along the river, Armstrong was heard by fledgling white musicians like trumpeter Bix Beiderbecke and trombonist Jack Teagarden, who would later become one of Armstrong's more celebrated sidemen.

In 1922, Armstrong got the call from Oliver to join his Creole Jazz Band as second cornetist. Armstrong hooked up with the band in Chicago but, upon hearing it play at a local nightclub, almost turned around and went back home because it sounded so good. He stayed and made a good band sound even better.

At first, Armstrong's big sound was held in by Oliver's tight New Orleans–style ensemble. But it didn't take long for the second cornetist to assert himself. In thirty-seven recordings made by the band in 1923, one can hear Armstrong's powerful voice taking shape in "Chimes Blues," "Dippermouth Blues," "Tears," and "Alligator Hop." He became the Creole Jazz Band's major attraction for his glittering solo breaks that thrilled audiences and inspired musicians.

With his legend growing in Chicago, Armstrong, at the urging of his then wife and Oliver band pianist Lil Hardin, left for New York in 1924 to take a job offered by bandleader Fletcher Henderson (1897–1952), who, with the help of arranger and lead saxophonist Don Redman (1900–1964), was bringing furious inventiveness to dance-band music.

Henderson had known about Armstrong since the lat-

King Oliver's Creole Jazz Band:
Honore Dutrey, trombone; Baby Dodds, drums;
King Oliver, cornet; Louis Armstrong, slide trumpet;
Lil Hardin, piano; Bill Johnson, banjo/bass;
Johnny Dodds, clarinet

ter's early days in New Orleans. But he may not have been prepared for the impact the new horn player would have on the band, even though it already included such clever improvisers as Redman and Coleman Hawkins. As he had with the Oliver band, Armstrong made a good band great, simply by asserting his radiant, robust style.

Armstrong returned to Chicago in 1925, ready to lead his own band. In November of that year, he made the first of sixty-five recordings on the Okeh label as leader of two recording ensembles known as the Hot Five and the Hot Seven. Both were New Orleans–style groups with a stronger emphasis on individual solos and rhythmic variations.

The February 1926 Hot Five recording session accidentally yielded one of the group's first innovations. While recording "Heebie Jeebies," Armstrong lost hold of the sheet music on the stand just as he was about to sing the vocals. On the spur of the moment, he began making up nonsense syllables to go along with the melody. It proved such an effective interlude that other musicians and singers began interjecting what became known as "scat singing" into their tunes.

"Cornet Chop Suey," "Struttin' with Some Barbecue," "Hotter Than That," "Potato Head Blues," "(I Want a) Big Butter and Egg Man," "S.O.L. Blues," and many more Hot Five/Hot Seven recordings featured Armstrong in the full bloom of his bravura powers. His improvisations with both his horn and his voice emerge as startling, yet logical extensions of the tunes he and his bandmates are playing. His tone on the horn is always clear, bright and bold. He knows how to relate to the beat. His approach to rhythm and riffing brought "swing" into jazz music.

Seventy years after these recordings were made, it is still possible to feel breathtaking excitement on first hearing, for instance, the stop-time breaks Armstrong takes on "Potato Head Blues." (A "stop-time" break is one in which a soloist sings or plays over a series of accents or rests.) Even more thrilling is the opening fanfare of "West End Blues," the 1928 Hot Five recording that, in critic Martin Williams's words, "represent[s] a beautiful balance of brilliant virtuosity and eloquent simplicity."[3]

That record was also the peak of Armstrong's year-long collaboration with pianist Earl Hines (1903–1983), who opened up vistas for jazz piano as vast as the frontiers Armstrong had expanded for all jazz music.

These records were wildly popular in their day, But few listeners thought they would be lasting art. In fact, jazz, and the Hot Five and Seven recordings in particular, drew the same mixture of condescension and condemnation that rock and rap would sustain in later years. Some regarded jazz records as corrupters of youth. When you hear the funny, insinuating, and seductive Armstrong-Hines collaboration "Tight Like That" (1928), you understand, if not appreciate, the concern.

"Tight Like That" was the last of the Hot Fives/Sevens recording sessions. But Armstrong stayed on a roll for at least the next five years. His fame grew beyond the jazz world with his appearance in a 1929 Broadway revue, playing and singing Fats Waller's "Ain't Misbehavin'." The success of his recording of that tune made him lean less on blues and more on pop tunes of the day, like "When You're Smiling," "Sweethearts on Parade," "I Can't Give You Anything but Love," "When It's Sleepy Time Down South," and "On the Sunny Side of the Street." Even the corniest of these tunes was given stature by Armstrong's performance.

It's hard to pick a high point of Armstrong's recordings between 1928 and 1933. One stunner was the dirge "Black and Blue." Originally written as a lovelorn lament, the song was transformed by Armstrong into protest music of such imposing grandeur that it inspired the African-American writer Ralph Ellison, almost twenty years later, to weave it into the preface of his novel *Invisible Man*. Other recordings of this period, "Basin Street Blues," "Memories of You," and "I Got a Right to Sing the Blues," resound today as definitive works by jazz's first virtuoso.

During this same period, Armstrong's impact as an entertainer was being felt as well. Inspired by the example of black tap dancer Bill "Bojangles" Robinson, Armstrong developed a stage personality that was, at once, commanding and nonthreatening, joyous and cagey, sly and infectious. This persona seduced audiences throughout the world. Yet from the 1930s onward, Armstrong would be criticized for what was viewed as overly effusive behavior. To many, he seemed to be having more fun onstage than a serious African-American artist should.

Armstrong made no apologies for this. He felt he had nothing to prove to anyone about being a proud black man. Nor did he hold any illusions about racism in America and abroad. His own experiences—from the time a white radio announcer refused to introduce him on the air in the 1930s, to the FBI surveillance placed on him after he publicly criticized President Eisenhower's slow responses in helping school integration in Little Rock, Arkansas, in 1957—kept him aware that the glory he'd earned since his days delivering coal in New Orleans couldn't shield him from discrimination and injustice.

Still Armstrong survived and, most times, prevailed over all kinds of trouble. When, in the early 1930s, he was caught in the middle of a mob war for his services, he simply kept clear of New York and Chicago for two years and went on performing on stages, in studios, and in films throughout Europe.

Controversy persists to this day over whether Armstrong had somehow compromised himself. Swing, bop, and other changes in jazz would move the music forward with Pops off to the side, playing and singing as he'd always done.

It may be true that, in later years, Armstrong became more institution than innovator, traveling the world as an

Louis Armstrong

ambassador of goodwill and guardian of traditional jazz. But as the recordings he made in the 1940s and 1950s clearly demonstrate, Armstrong didn't *play* like a statue. Well into his fifties and sixties, Armstrong was still capable of playing with the same deceptive simplicity and stark purity he'd shown in his youth. And he could still sell records! He had a hit in 1964 ("Hello, Dolly!"), seven years before his death in 1971. He had another ("What a Wonderful World," recorded in 1966) in 1989, eighteen years after.

How important was he? The answer is as far away as the nearest radio. Every jazz player, from Lester Young and Miles Davis to Ornette Coleman and Wynton Marsalis, owes Pops big time. So does every pop singer, from Bing Crosby and Frank Sinatra to Elvis Presley and Michael Jackson. Even the Beatles—nudged from the top of the charts in May 1964 by Armstrong's "Hello, Dolly!"—wouldn't have been possible without the risks Armstrong had taken forty years before.

five

SWING BECOMES THE THING

ONCE LOUIS ARMSTRONG opened the frontier, there was no turning back. Arrangers and composers were inspired to devise blues and pop tunes with more melodic and rhythmic range. Soloists were challenged to become as inventive in their own playing as Pops was in his. All this activity would reshape jazz, loosening its rhythms, diversfying its tones and phrases well beyond what the New Orleans masters could imagine.

By the mid-1930s, all these developments were collected under one word: *swing*. This word is used, to this day, to describe a hard-driving rhythmic momentum in music. Its presence is felt in everything from contemporary jazz to country-western music. No one has come up with a precise definition of swing. But almost everyone knows it when they hear it.

The seeds for swing were planted in Armstrong's 1924 tenure with the Fletcher Henderson orchestra. It was, as noted in the last chapter, a brief one. (One of the reasons

The Fletcher Henderson Band:
(From left) Howard Scott, trumpet; Coleman Hawkins, tenor sax;
Louis Armstrong, trumpet; Charlie Dixon, banjo;
Fletcher Henderson, piano; Kaiser Marshall, drums;
Buster Bailey, clarinet/alto sax;
Elmer Chambers, trumpet;
Charlie Green, trombone; Ralph Escudero, tuba;
Don Redman, alto sax/arranger

he left, Armstrong later said, was that Henderson wouldn't let him sing on records.) But he was with New York's hottest black band long enough to excite every musician who saw him play.

Both Henderson and his arranger Don Redman realized that Armstrong's riffs and rhythmic daring could be absorbed into an orchestra's sound. And it wasn't long after Armstrong returned to Chicago that the band was displaying Armstrong's influence, especially in the solos by saxophonist Coleman Hawkins and cornetists Joe Smith and Rex Stewart (Armstrong's replacement).

It's hard to tell from recordings of the Henderson band from that period what made it so innovative and popular. The oom-pah rhythms sound clunky and repetitive. (You understand why so many dance tunes of the twenties were called "stomps.") But much of the big band music setting the tone for the 1930s would have been impossible without Henderson.

Born in Georgia, James Fletcher Henderson graduated from Atlanta University with a degree in chemistry. He went north to New York in 1920 to do postgraduate work. But he drifted into the city's music scene, playing piano with W. C. Handy, Bessie Smith and Ethel Waters. In 1923, his first big band appeared at the Club Alabam and, the following year, at the famous Roseland Ballroom, where the Henderson band would enjoy steady work for the next ten years.

Rex Stewart remembered Henderson, often called "Smack," as "a man of imposing stature, about six feet two or so. His complexion was that of an octoroon and in his youth he could have been mistaken for an Italian. . . . He could be frivolous or serious, according to his mood. However, even in his zany moments, there would be overtones of gentility."[1]

Redman, who joined the band shortly after its Club Alabam engagement, was, in contrast to the leader, "short-statured, brown-skinned."[2] Also unlike Henderson, Redman had been absorbed in music all his life. He could play the trumpet at three, joined a band at six, and was thoroughly schooled in theory, harmony, and composition. "He played a mean alto [saxophone]," it was said of Redman, "and sang in a soft, almost ethereal whisper."[3]

The four years that Redman worked as Henderson's arranger yielded many innovations in orchestral jazz, especially after Armstrong left New York. Some of the boldness Armstrong brought to his playing emerged in such Redman charts as "The Stampede" (1926) and "Variety Stomp" (1927). In both tunes, there were passages written so that sections of the band seem to be talking back and forth to each other. Like many innovations, this "call-and-response" pattern had deep roots in black musical history.

To hear recordings of the Henderson band during Redman's arranging tenure is like witnessing a furious experiment in mixing and matching tones, riffs, and musical personalities. Witnesses to the period say the band's vitality was best appreciated in live performances, rather than from the records of that period. Musicians, especially, were challenged by the roaring bravado of Henderson's orchestra. "When I first formed a big band in New York," Duke Ellington later recalled, "[Henderson's] was the one I wanted mine to sound like."[4]

Given Henderson's success, he should have been dubbed the "king of jazz," at least in New York City. But in an era when racial segregation was taken for granted as the American way of life, Paul Whiteman held that title, leading successful all-white bands whose music mixed jazz syncopation with symphonic-style orchestrations. (Henderson, meanwhile, was called the "colored king of jazz.")

In retrospect, Whiteman's bands of the 1920s were less distinguished for their music than for their musicians. Cornetists Bix Beiderbecke and Red Nichols, saxophonists

Jimmy Dorsey and Frank Trumbauer, Dorsey's trombonist brother Tommy, guitarist Eddie Lang, violinist Joe Venuti were among those who passed through the ranks of Whiteman's band, achieving renown and influence independent of Whiteman's own.

Of these, Beiderbecke (1903–1931) was the best known and loved. Both his plaintive, lyric horn playing and his untimely death at twenty-eight, of pneumonia complicated by alcoholism, have given him mythic status in jazz history. His cornet playing was lighter-toned, less robust and more introspective, than Armstrong's. But musicians everywhere, Armstrong included, were captivated by the striking originality of Beiderbecke's solos in such tunes as "Davenport Blues" and "Singin' the Blues."

Frank Trumbauer, whose smooth lyricism influenced such saxophonists as Johnny Hodges, Benny Carter, and Lester Young, was the principal player in the Jean Goldkette band, a little-remembered, but influential white orchestra that featured many imaginative arrangements and soloists. Rex Stewart later described the Goldkette band as "without question . . . the first original white swing band in history." Indeed, they swung so hard at a 1927 Roseland engagement that Stewart, along with the rest of the Fletcher Henderson band present that night, remembers feeling "amazed, angry, morose, and bewildered."[5] To use the expression jazz musicians use when competing with each other, Goldkette's outfit had "cut" Henderson's.

In 1928, Henderson's band faced more troubling developments. Redman left the orchestra and took his arranging talents to McKinney's Cotton Pickers. Later that year, Henderson was injured in an automobile accident while traveling through Kentucky with members of the band. "He had an awful hit in his head and his left shoulder was pushed over to his collarbone," Henderson's wife, Leora, later recalled. "Believe me, Fletcher was never the same after that."[6]

Meanwhile, much of what Henderson and his band had started was being extended by bands throughout America. One of the best was led by Jimmy Lunceford (1902–1947), who studied music in Denver under Paul Whiteman's father and went on to earn degrees in music from Fisk University and New York's City College. He taught high school music in Memphis, where he started organizing a band from the ranks of his students in the late 1920s. By the early thirties, Lunceford's band had become one of the prototypes of early swing. Arranger, trumpeter, and vocalist Sy Oliver (1910–1988) signed on with Lunceford in 1933, bringing added wit and sophistication to a band already celebrated for its discipline and showmanship.

Bands throughout the country, white and black, were following the trail Henderson had blazed. But for the trailblazer himself, things indeed were "never the same" after the 1928 accident. His zest for bandleading seemed to fall off. His band found engagements and recording gigs hard to come by in an America whose economy, after the 1929 stock market crash, would be hit hard by the Great Depression.

Henderson's roster of players remained impressive during the early 1930s: from stalwarts like Stewart, Coleman Hawkins, and bassist John Kirby, to newcomers like arranger-saxophonist Benny Carter, trumpeters Henry "Red" Allen and Bobby Stark, and saxophonist Ben Webster.

But Coleman Hawkins was coming into his own as an important improviser. In 1934 he left the band to work in Europe, where jazz was finding wildly enthusiastic audiences. His departure was a blow from which the Henderson band couldn't recover. Financial problems forced Henderson, later that year, to sell some of his arrangements to an orchestra headed by clarinetist Benny Goodman (1909–1986), a white, Chicago-born virtuoso.

Goodman's first break came with the Ben Pollack

orchestra, with which he made his first recording in 1926. When the band moved to New York, Goodman became a successful free-lance musician, playing in Broadway pit orchestras, studio recording sessions, and radio shows. In 1934, with help from the record producer and impresario John Hammond, Goodman organized his first jazz orchestra. That spring, the band was given a spot on a weekly radio show, "Let's Dance."

Henderson's charts for "Basin Street Blues," "Blue Skies," and, especially, the Jelly Roll Morton standard "King Porter Stomp," set the pace for the swing phenomenon. The combination of these arrangements with dynamic players like trumpeter Bunny Berigan (1908–1942) and drummer Gene Krupa (1909–1973) proved hugely popular on records. Just how popular was made clear at an August 1935 performance in Los Angeles, where crowds of young people responded to the band's fast-moving sound with the kind of hysteria that would greet a young Frank Sinatra the following decade. And Elvis Presley the decade after that. And the Beatles after that.

To his everlasting credit, Goodman, more than any white bandleader who preceded him, appreciated the contributions made to the success of swing by African-American musicians like Henderson. The same year as the Los Angeles explosion, Goodman used his newfound fame to break down racial barriers by fielding an all-star small combo featuring Krupa and black pianist Teddy Wilson (1912–1986).

The trio became a quartet the following year with the addition of black vibraphonist Lionel Hampton (1909–), who made his first splash on the instrument in Louis Armstrong's memorable 1930 recording of "Memories of You." The quartet—later a sextet, with white bassist Arthur Bernstein and black guitarist Charlie Christian—was a model of small-ensemble jazz.

By the late 1930s, both Krupa and Hampton had

The Benny Goodman Sextet, with Lionel Hampton:
Fletcher Henderson, piano; Charlie Christian, guitar;
Nick Fatool, drums; Lionel Hampton, vibraphone;
Artie Bernstein, bass; Benny Goodman, clarinet

organized big bands of their own. The star instrumentalist of Krupa's orchestra, besides the drummer himself, was black trumpeter Roy Eldridge (1911–1989), whose daredevil speed runs on his horn's upper register extended Armstrong's inventions while inspiring trumpet players who would bring about jazz's next transformation.

Hampton, who had done much to expand the vibraphone's role in jazz, formed several small "pickup" bands while with the Goodman combo. These bands included some of the best musicians of the period and few such units were as stellar as the group that recorded "When Lights Are Low" in 1939. Tenor saxophonists Coleman Hawkins, Ben Webster, and Chu Berry; drummer Cozy Cole; and the remarkable Charlie Christian on guitar, combined to make a classic.

The key player in this session, as soloist and as arranger, was Benny Carter (1907–), who had a busy decade playing alto saxophone and trumpet, and arranging pieces for McKinney's Cotton Pickers and the bands of Henderson and drummer Chick Webb before forming his own band in 1933. Two years later, he went to Europe, where he worked as an arranger with the BBC and as director of an interracial band at a Dutch seaside resort. He returned to the States in 1938 to restart his band. Respected and accomplished as a leader and arranger, Carter was also famed for his lucid, imaginative, and intelligent soloing on the alto sax. Now in his late eighties, Carter remains active on records and in live performances.

Indeed, although big bands dominated the 1930s, the era was just as significant for great improvisers like Eldridge and Carter. There was, for instance, Art Tatum (1910–1956), whose amazing speed and virtuosity on the piano were all the more remarkable for his being virtually blind. (He was born in Toledo, Ohio, with partial vision in his one "good" eye.) After making a name for himself as a radio performer in his hometown, he went to New York in 1932 to accompany singer Adelaide Hall. His first recorded solos the following year created a sensation in the jazz world, especially among pianists, who were astonished by Tatum's amazing technique.

Tatum wasn't *all* style. His early 1940s recordings with blues singer Big Joe Turner (1911–1985) prove he could play a simple blues chorus with restraint, while applying his own striking tone colors and rhythmic embellishments. If jazz improvisers tell stories with music, then Tatum, who put as much into his narratives as his imagination allowed, was among the best ever.

When the story of singer Billie Holiday (1915–1959) is told, emphasis is always placed on the heartbreak and torment of her personal life. Born Eleanora Fagan in Philadelphia, Holiday grew up in Baltimore. Her parents never married. She seldom saw her father, Clarence Holliday, who played banjo and guitar with the Fletcher Henderson band in the late twenties and early thirties. Her famous memoir, *Lady Sings the Blues*, recounts a childhood of abuse from relatives who helped raise her. As a teenager, she was caught up in a scene of hustlers, prostitutes, and all-night music. She went to New York in 1930 and sang in Harlem clubs. At one place, Benny Goodman and John Hammond heard her sing. She made her first record, with Goodman, in 1933.

It was often said of Holiday that she "sang her life." And it's hard not to feel, when hearing her more plaintive, poignant singing, some of the pain and torment. Her addiction to alcohol and drugs, her bad breaks with love and the law are elements that have contributed to a romantic myth, dyed in deep blue, that influences people's reactions to her singing. The sorrow was genuine. Yet it was also as much a part of Holiday's public image as the gardenia she wore in

Billie Holiday

her hair for a performance. Many of her devoted fans found solace in connecting with her pain, which some believed was what made her an artist.

But while Holiday's singing—her art—reflected her troubles, it didn't directly emerge *from* them. Even in her later years, when her performances became erratic and her luck turned worse, Holiday's vocals were gestures of defiance against despair. These days, many listeners hear in Holiday's singing a joy in pure creation that is as infectious as what is heard in the music of Louis Armstrong, who, along with Bessie Smith, was a role model for Holiday.

Throughout the 1930s, Holiday made a series of recordings with some of the greatest jazz musicians of her day. Like Armstrong, she was able to take an ordinary pop melody and transform it with a mixture of subtle, declarative power and clever, intuitive phrasing into a jazz classic.

In the 1940s, Holiday moved her listeners with such socially conscious songs as "Strange Fruit," white composer Lewis Allen's lament about the lynching of black men in the South, and Holiday's own "God Bless the Child." Her ongoing problems with narcotics and the law were exacting a physical toll on her, and the emotional scars can be detected on her 1950s performances.

But many listeners believe Holiday's twilight recordings, even with the occasional vocal cracks and missed lyrics, represent a different kind of triumph. It was as if, during these final years, there was a battle between Holiday's intepretive imagination and mortality's icy grip. Mortality scored a victory in the end. But not before Holiday got in a few sharp blows of her own.

In the annals of jazz, Ella Fitzgerald (1917–) is often set up as Holiday's polar opposite. It's true that the exuberance seen in Fitzgerald's image contrasts sharply with the somber cloak that seems always to drape Holiday's persona. And while Holiday's inventions depend on relatively few notes, Fitzgerald is regarded as the grand diva of scat.

It's when comparisons are broadened to artistic judgments that things get ridiculous. Because of the comparative lack of high drama in her personal life, Fitzgerald is viewed by some as a lesser singer than Holiday. But Fitzgerald's vocal agility and virtuosity are buttressed by strong stuff. She has been as effective a dramatist as any vocalist or instrumentalist in jazz music. She can deal with a variety of moods, tempos, and musical genres with conviction. And as her long career testifies, she has the energy to match her great warmth.

Fitzgerald's big break came in 1934 when, at sixteen, she won a talent show at Harlem's Apollo Theater. Drummer-bandleader Chick Webb hired her a year later. She had a string of pop hits with the Webb band, notably a 1938 version of the nursery rhyme "A Tisket, A Tasket." Webb died of tuberculosis of the spine in 1939. Fitzgerald continued to lead the band for a year afterward before going solo.

From the beginning, Fitzgerald's singing was marked by hornlike clarity and an impeccable grasp of rhythm. These were legacies of the swing era, and they have carried Fitzgerald through several musical epochs. Her own greatest legacy may be the series of recordings she made in the 1950s of "songbooks" devoted to the works of popular composers like Cole Porter, George and Ira Gershwin, Irving Berlin, Harold Arlen, and Johnny Mercer. Others make a case for the 1950s and 1960s recordings of live concerts where she never failed to take off on dazzling, sustained runs of scatting and paraphrasing. In either case, it's difficult to find a jazz singer worthy of the name—male or female, black, white, or whatever—who doesn't carry pieces of either Holiday or Fitzgerald with him or her.

One name that has come up frequently in this chapter

*Ella Fitzgerald
with Ray Brown, bass,
and Dizzy Gillespie*

is Coleman Hawkins (1909–1969), whom musicians called "Bean." He was the stalwart tenor saxophonist of Fletcher Henderson's bands of the twenties and early thirties. By the time he left for Europe in 1934, he had become the preeminent player on his instrument (though others, like Chu Berry, Lester Young, and Herschel Evans, were serious challengers).

Hawkins had originally intended to stay overseas briefly. But, like Benny Carter and other black musicians who visited Europe, Hawkins found wildly appreciative audiences for his bold improvisations. He played with Carter, the French Gypsy guitarist Django Reinhardt, and many others on the Continent before returning to the United States in 1939 and forming a nine-piece band. This was the unit that, in the same year, recorded what would become one of the most influential and celebrated jazz instrumental records of all time.

"Body and Soul" was a 1930 pop ballad performed by many vocalists and instrumentalists. The way they recorded such a ballad, at whatever tempo, was to state the melody at the beginning and stay close to it throughout, no matter how fancy it got. Hawkins went against the grain. On his version of "Body and Soul," you never hear the melody played straight. His solo leans entirely on the song's harmonies. That would have been innovative enough. But the passionate phrases Hawkins draws from his saxophone deliver the emotional punch of this recording, which was a culmination of what Armstrong started—and a harbinger of what was to come.

Hawkins's former boss, Fletcher Henderson, continued to write arrangements for Goodman and for swing orchestras like the Dorsey brothers'. He kept trying to sustain a band of his own through the 1940s, collecting, writing, and performing gigs here and there before suffering a stroke in 1950 that left him bedridden. He died two years later.

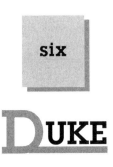

DUKE

HOW DO YOU account for genius? It helped, Duke Ellington would later say, to have been "spoiled rotten" as a child.

Born in Washington, D.C., Edward Kennedy Ellington (1899–1974) was told constantly by his mother, Daisy, "Edward you are blessed. You don't have anything to worry about. Edward, you are blessed."[1] His father, James, worked as a servant for a prominent local doctor. He taught Ellington the value of good manners, fine clothes, and graceful deportment. In their respective ways, both parents gave Ellington the serene confidence and aristocratic bearing that would beguile the world and support his art.

Formal music training never set well with young Ellington, who seemed destined for a career in commercial art. As a boy, however, Ellington was so inspired by the ragtime pianists working all over D.C. that he began to play rags himself, mostly by ear. While still in his early teens, he began to write music. It was about the same time that another youth, acknowledging Ellington's precocious savoir faire, endowed young Edward with the regal nick-name—Duke—that he would wear for the rest of his life.

He dropped out of high school in 1917 to play music gigs at night while working at different jobs by day. He got to hear pianists like Luckey Roberts, Eubie Blake, and James P. Johnson, whose "Carolina Shout" Ellington mastered by playing along with the piano roll. By 1919, Ellington had formed his own band, The Duke's Serenaders. Gradually, both he and the band expanded their musical horizons beyond ragtime and his hometown. He left for New York in 1923, with a pair of musical comrades, saxophonist-bassist Otto Hardwick and drummer Sonny Greer.

After a shaky start with the Wilbur Sweatman orches-tra, the trio hooked up with a fellow Washingtonian, band-leader-banjoist Elmer Snowden, who was leading a band called the Washingtonians. Ellington, Greer, Hardwick, and Snowden were soon joined by James "Bubber" Miley (1903–1932), a horn player influenced by King Oliver's use of mutes to create a near-vocal effect.

Gradually, Ellington assumed command of the Washingtonians after Snowden left the group, and Fred Guy took the banjo-guitar chair. In 1925, the group secured an engagement at a midtown Manhattan nightclub called the Hollywood, which, after being destroyed by fire, was rebuilt and renamed Club Kentucky.

Fletcher Henderson's band was ruling the nearby Roseland Ballroom at the same time. Ellington admired that orchestra's dazzling horn arrangements and foot-stomping rhythms. At the Kentucky, Ellington began to build on what Henderson and Redman had done. He sculpted arrange-ments that allowed greater room for soloists like Miley and Hardwick, saxophonist Harry Carney (1910–1974), and trombonist Joe "Tricky Sam" Nanton (1904–1946) to express their distinctive instrumental voices. At the same time, these voices would enhance the meaning and mood of whatever the orchestra, as a whole, was playing. This dynamic balance of individual and collective expression soon made Ellington's band sound like no other in New York—or anywhere else.

While still at the Kentucky, Ellington's reputation spread through recordings and radio dates. In December 1927, the ensemble got its big break: an extended engagement at the Cotton Club, a glamorous, gangster-owned Harlem nightclub open only to whites and the most celebrated blacks. Meanwhile, blacks were the only ones performing onstage and working backstage.

The club was known for its elaborate and exotic stage shows. For an instinctual dramatist like Ellington, these shows offered a perfect match for such quirky pieces as "East St. Louis Toodle-oo" (which immortalized Bubber Miley's growling, plunger-assisted horn playing), "Creole Love Call" (which contains a plaintive vocal with no lyrics, an Ellington specialty), "The Mooche," "Black and Tan Fantasy," "Rockin' in Rhythm," and his first commercial hit, "Mood Indigo."

"Jungle music" was what much of Ellington's music was called during his six years at the Cotton Club. Yet the audacity of Ellington's pieces, the sophistication of his arrangements, and, most important, his perfection of the delicate balance of soloist and ensemble in a jazz piece, combined to transcend the derogatory "jungle" label—and jazz itself.

The Cotton Club made Ellington a household name, partly through its live weekly radio broadcasts. His band also appeared in films like the 1929 short *Black and Tan*. During the late 1920s, the Ellington band acquired valuable new players. In 1927, Barney Bigard (1906–1980), a clarinetist from New Orleans, joined the band's reed section. Alto saxophonist Johnny Hodges (1907–1970), whom many came to view as the orchestra's heart and soul, arrived the following year.

Miley, Ellington's first big star, left the band in 1929. His replacement, Charles "Cootie" Williams (1911–1985), lacked Miley's bluster, but brought his own emotional power. Juan Tizol (1900–1984), who joined in 1929, and Lawrence Brown, who joined in 1932, added their idiosyncratic voices to Nanton's in the trombone section. These men, along with Greer and Carney, who had become jazz's leading baritone saxophonists, gave Ellington much to work with.

As the raucous 1920s became the desperate 1930s, it was becoming apparent to jazz aficionados and musicians alike that Ellington was more than the leader of a dance band. After all, most dance bands, even the best, merely attached themes to appropriate rhythms. Ellington "played" his orchestra the way his musicians played their instruments. He used his distinctive performers to tell stories, to paint emotional landscapes with sound. (The comparison is especially apt for the onetime art student who never completely abandoned his paints.)

In 1933, the band left for a European tour. Their appearance at the London Palladium broke all previous box-office records. That his music was both loved *and* appreciated by European audiences encouraged Ellington to conceive more adventurous pieces like "Daybreak Express," "Rude Interlude," and "Blue Harlem." Meanwhile, hits like "Sophisticated Lady," "Solitude," and "In a Sentimental Mood" were played and sung throughout the country.

The band benefited from the swing movement gathering momentum in the mid-1930s. (Indeed, Benny Goodman included a tribute to Ellington's music at the January 1938 Carnegie Hall concert that certified the swing era.) But Ellington was following his own path in music and wanted no part of categories like "swing," "jazz," or "pop" to define what he was doing. Indeed, the maestro's highest praise for a musician he enjoyed was the expression "beyond category."

By the late 1930s, Ellington's prodigious creativity was pulling the orchestra to further greatness. There were some key personnel adjustments during this period. Rex Stewart

The Duke Ellington Band at the Cotton Club:
Wellman Braud, bass; Joe Nanton, trombone;
Juan Tizol, valve trombone/arranger;
Otto Hardwick, alto sax; Lawrence Brown, trombone;
Harry Carney, baritone sax; Sonny Greer, drums;
Cootie Williams, trumpet; Johnny Hodges, alto and suprano sax;
Duke Ellington, piano/arranger; Arthur Whetsol, trumpet;
Barney Bigard, clarinet/tenor sax;
Freddie Jenkins, trumpet; Fred Guy, guitar

brought his lean, witty horn phrases to the band in 1934. Tenor saxophonist Ben Webster (1909–1973) was in the band on-and-off in the mid-1930s. When he signed on full-time in 1939, his bristly passionate lyricism flourished as never before.

In that same year, there were two more crucial additions: bassist Jimmy Blanton (1918–1942) and composer-arranger Billy Strayhorn (1915–1967). Before the twenty-one-year-old Blanton arrived, the bass in a jazz orchestra did little more than keep the rhythm going. By the time of his untimely death from tuberculosis, he had given his instrument a melodic voice.

The scholarly-looking Strayhorn shared Ellington's grand ambitions for orchestral jazz. His charts and compositions were as inspired as the maestro's. Sometimes Strayhorn himself conducted the orchestra or played the piano in Ellington's place. He was more than just an assistant and consultant to Ellington. He was his alter ego. Years later, Ellington would refer to him as "my right arm, my left arm, all the eyes in the back of my head, my brain waves in his head, his in mine."[3]

With Strayhorn, Blanton, and Webster in place, musical history was about to be made. Between 1940 and 1942, this edition of the Ellington band recorded what has been called some of the finest music of the twentieth century. Two masterpieces were recorded in March 1940. "Ko-Ko" can still take your breath away as it starts out with a low roar and builds to the kind of climactic rush you get from a good suspense movie. "Concerto for Cootie" is the other masterpiece. The piece was better known in later years as "Do Nothing Till You Hear from Me." It is, in this early form, an, elegant conversation between the orchestra and trumpeter Williams (the "Cootie" in the title).

As he had from the beginning, Ellington wrote pieces that brought out the best in his soloists. Later in 1940, "Never No Lament" (which would become better known as "Don't Get Around Much Anymore") was recorded with Johnny Hodges's alto sax bending the melody with volup-

Duke Ellington (left) with Billy Strayhorn

tuous grace. Hodges's and Williams's inventiveness were also evident in another easygoing swinger from that year, "In a Mellowtone."

Strayhorn, meanwhile, came into his own as a composer in early 1941 with "Take the A Train," which became the band's theme song and offered a debut solo for trumpeter-violinist Ray Nance (1913–1976). Nance's irrepressible humor became another strength Ellington and Strayhorn could call upon when they needed to evoke an emotion or mood. It seemed as if every musician's instrument was an actor in whatever dramas or character sketches Ellington and his aide devised. Because, for instance, Hodges and Webster had the more luxurious tones, they got most of the romantic-lead parts, while Nanton, a master with both the plunger and the mute, got to be funny or sad depending on the theme. Virtuosos like Bigard and Blanton could play whatever role was handed them.

During these years, Ellington also wrote many long and short pieces with themes rooted in black culture. "Harlem Air Shaft," recorded in 1940, sounded like a raucous Harlem apartment building—with a simple horn riff acting as its sturdy foundation. In 1941, Ellington wrote much of the music for a revue production, "Jump for Joy," intended to both celebrate black culture and protest its debasement by American society.

At the orchestra's 1943 Carnegie Hall concert, Ellington unveiled his most ambitious work to that point: a suite celebrating black America in all its complexity and richness, entitled "Black, Brown, and Beige." Ellington was disappointed in the lukewarm reception to the piece, and later Carnegie Hall concerts featured pieces that were just as neglected. The biting "Deep South Suite" was unveiled in 1946, the December 1947 concert featured the "Liberian Suite" and the haunting "The Clothed Woman," a short piece for piano.

By 1943, Blanton was dead. Bigard, Williams, and Webster were gone. And though the latter two would return, a drought of hits and greater turnover of band members would begin by the mid-1940s and last for nearly a decade. Through it all, Ellington continued writing and recording with such emerging stars as trumpeter Clark Terry (1920–), bassist Oscar Pettiford (1922–1960), drummer Louis Bellson (1924–), and tenor saxophonist Paul Gonsalves (1920–1974). Historians and music archivists are discovering many outstanding recordings from this period, still regarded by some as a low point in Ellington's career.

The "comeback" happened in dramatic fashion at the 1956 Newport Jazz Festival, when a thrilling set by the Ellington band was climaxed by a performance of Ellington's "Diminuendo and Crescendo in Blue," bridged by a twenty-seven-chorus solo by Gonsalves. The audience was electrified into a near-frenzy. Ellington appeared on the cover of *Time* magazine. Duke was big-time once again.

Ellington found himself busy from that time on. His band's road schedule was hectic and global. Meanwhile, he wrote film scores for *Anatomy of a Murder* (1959) and *Paris Blues* (1962) and worked with Strayhorn on albums like "Such Sweet Thunder," a 1957 suite of works inspired by Shakespeare's plays. Strayhorn's death from cancer ten years later devastated Ellington, who continued to make great recordings—including a moving tribute to his aide, "And His Mother Called Him Bill" (1967).

Much of the music Ellington wrote in his last years was in the sacred vein: masses, hymns, and swing tunes with biblical themes like "The Shepherd." Honors were bestowed on him from every country, including his own. He received a Presidential Medal of Freedom in a 1969 White House reception marking his seventieth birthday. "There is no place I would rather be than in my mother's arms," Ellington said before kissing President Richard M. Nixon twice on both cheeks. "Why four times?" the bewildered Nixon asked. "One for each cheek," Ellington replied.[4]

When the maestro died in May 1974, his eulogists said he belonged in the company of European masters like Beethoven, Mozart, and Bach. Just as he belongs in the company of an inventive, prodigious painter like Picasso, or an expansive, worldly dramatist like Shakespeare. Genius is the one category for the man who believed that music came only in two categories: good and bad.

seven

THE COUNT, THE PREZ, AND THE K.C. SOUND

FATE PLAYED what seemed, at first, to be a dirty trick on twenty-three-year-old Bill Basie when it tossed him in the middle of Kansas City, Missouri, with no immediate way of getting out. It was 1927 and Basie (1904–1984) was a couple of thousand miles from his birthplace in Red Bank, New Jersey.

His mother taught him music. He learned how to "stride" on the piano from the Harlem masters James P. Johnson, Willie "the Lion" Smith, and Fats Waller, who also taught Basie how to coax the blues out of an organ. Basie had become good enough to get pianist jobs with traveling vaudeville shows. But in Kansas City the money ran out on one tour, leaving Basie with no job, no money, and no immediate prospects. "I knew I couldn't do any good by sitting around feeling sorry for myself or wishing I'd never left my home in Red Bank," Basie later recalled.[1] So he looked around town for something to do.

Basie's luck was better than he realized at the time. In those years Kansas City was a "wide-open" town where gambling, bootlegging, racketeering, and all manner of vice flourished as in few other American cities, even at the peak of the "roaring twenties." Dance halls and nightclubs offered plenty of steady work for black musicians.

But, Bill Basie was without connections in this scene. So he spent a year playing piano in the pit of a silent-movie theater. In 1928, he hooked up with a prominent local band, the Blue Devils, which was led by bassist Walter Page (1900–1957). Trained in music at Kansas University, Page was as much teacher as he was leader of his talented band members, who included, at one time or another, singer Jimmy Rushing (1903–1972), trumpeter Oran "Hot Lips" Page (1908–1954), and a startling young tenor saxophonist named Lester Young (1909–1959).

The year Bill Basie signed up, the Blue Devils had become maybe the best of the so-called "territory bands" playing in dance halls throughout Kansas, Oklahoma, and Texas. Legend has it that one evening in 1928, the Blue Devils, who often engaged in musical duels with other Kansas City bands, seriously "smoked" (defeated) a group led by pianist Bennie Moten (1894–1935), whose own band was believed to be the Devils' only serious competition.

Moten, the legend continues, was so bruised by the Devils' victory that he started recruiting some Blue Devils to his own outfit. What gave Moten leverage was the fact that his band had, by the late 1920s, already established itself beyond the "territory" with steady work, New York bookings, and a recording contract. Basie and Rushing were among the first to sign with Moten. "Lips" Page soon followed, as did Walter Page. By 1933, when what was left of the band finally folded, the Blue Devils were absorbed into Moten's band.

Before the Devils' arrival, Moten's music tended to resemble a New Orleans ensemble, only with a heavier beat. Basie and trombonist-guitarist-arranger Eddie Durham (1906–1987) helped guide the Moten orchestra to the more fluid sound that would define Kansas City swing.

By the early 1930s, the Great Depression had settled in. But there were still plenty of good times to be had in Kansas City. Forty dance halls and dozens of nightclubs kept black musicians working till the wee hours of the morning. And the music would go on longer at marathon jam sessions, lasting till sunrise. Drummer Jo Jones (1911–1985), who arrived in Kansas City in 1933, later recalled, "You could be sleeping one morning at 6 A.M. and a traveling band would come into town for a few hours and would wake you up to make a couple hours' session until eight in the morning."[2]

There were many great bands playing what would be remembered as "some of the best blues and jazz to be heard anywhere in America."[3] One of the premier units, the Twelve Clouds of Joy, was led by bass saxophonist Andy Kirk (1898–1992) and featured a young piano prodigy from Pittsburgh named Mary Lou Williams (1910–1981), who, soon after joining the band in 1929, became its chief arranger and star soloist. "It was the first time we had ever seen a girl cat who could carve the local boys," recalled one rival bandleader.[4]

Despite the presence of bands like Kirk's, Bennie Moten's band ruled the Kansas City jazz scene between 1929 and 1933. Part of the reason was its leader's connection with Tom Pendergast, the corrupt political boss of Kansas City; also, the caliber of musicians Moten had at his disposal was formidable. Rushing's muscular singing and Lips Page's blistering trumpet attack were considerable assets. But it was the rhythm section of drummer Willie McWashington, bassist Walter Page, guitarist Eddie Durham, and the pianist now known as "Count" Basie, whose tempos set loose both the imagination of soloists and the feet of dance hall patrons.

In mid-December 1932, the Moten band reached the

low point of its energy—and the peak of its artistry. It was a drab winter's day and the band—broke, hungry, and near exhaustion—assembled at the RCA Victor recording studio in Camden, New Jersey, for a marathon recording session. Fortified only by bread and a pot of rabbit stew, the band put forth some of the best music of the era. One tune in particular, "Moten Swing," was a hard-driving model of Kansas City swing.

The repeal of Prohibition in 1933 was the beginning of the end of Kansas City's "wide-open" era. Even for Moten's band, gigs became scarce and many players briefly split with the leader over a wage dispute. They returned and Moten still ruled the Kansas City scene until one morning in early 1935 when he died on an operating table in the midst of a botched tonsillectomy.

Moten's brother, Buster, immediately took command of the band. But later that summer, Count Basie, who some in the band considered its true leader even before Moten's death, started his own band. Many key Moten stalwarts went with him, including Durham, Walter Page, and arranger Buster Smith. The Basie band soon found a regular gig at Kansas City's Reno Club, which broadcast the band's Sunday night performances throughout the Midwest.

One Reno Club broadcast was heard in 1936 by writer-producer-impresario John Hammond while he was traveling with Benny Goodman's band. Struck by the band's vitality, Hammond met with Basie and suggested he add four players to make the eight-piece ensemble a twelve-piece big band. By then, Lester Young had become the band's star player and Jo Jones's drumming proved a worthy compliment to Page and Basie.

Hammond, with help from Goodman's booking agent, put the band on a nationwide tour. Audiences were cool at first to the rough-and-tumble Basie sound. But by the time the band opened at New York's Roseland Ballroom in December 1936, it was starting to catch on. The following month, the Count Basie Orchestra began recording under its own name. It was those recordings that, gradually, made the band nationally famous.

In July 1937, the orchestra recorded what became its theme. "One O'Clock Jump" had been assembled two years earlier, when Basie's men were still stationed at the Reno Club. It had another, lewder title, but when it was broadcast from the club late one night, the radio announcer told Basie he couldn't read the name over the air. Basie looked at the clock, saw it was 1:00 A.M. and invented another title.[4]

The first recording of "Jump" begins with a couple of rolling piano choruses by Basie to set the pace. Then Herschel Evans comes in with a tenor solo sax set against a pulsating brass riff. Trombonist George Hunt takes the next chorus. Lester Young slides in for twelve bars of smooth lyricism. Trumpeter Buck Clayton makes a declarative statement, giving way to a Walter Page bass break. Then the whole band drives the tune the rest of the way home, piling riff upon riff toward a rousing crescendo.

By the time "One O'Clock Jump" was recorded, guitarist Freddie Green (1911–1987) had been added to the orchestra's roster. Together, Green, Basie, Page, and Jones rounded out the great rhythm section that drove the band to even greater glories. "Sent for You Yesterday," "Jumpin' at the Woodside," "Doggin' Around," "Swing'n the Blues," "Lady Be Good," "Dickie's Dream," "Lester Leaps In"—all these became immediate hits and enduring classics. Each was typified by a solid rhythmic pulse and spare phrasing from Basie's piano.

Such designs were wide-open enough to allow the band's soloists to not only add their own flourishes but to project their own personalities onto the tunes. Through this process, they became stars. None glowed brighter than Lester Young, the brilliant, enigmatic player everyone called "the president of the tenor saxophone"—or "Prez" for short.

Like the Basie band, Young didn't catch on immediately with the public. Coleman Hawkins's thick, lustrous tone was, for many, the way a jazz tenor saxophone should sound. Young's tone was thinner and softer. This seemed to allow him to convey a wider range of emotion and invention than anything Hawkins—or, for that matter, Louis Armstrong himself—had attempted.

There was something both flamboyant and laid-back about the way Young uncoiled his lyrical phrases in the midst of Basie's tough orchestrations, seemingly without breaking a sweat. His most characteristic playing stance had his saxophone tipped on an angle. He seemed both distant from and engaged in the main action of the band, in the manner of a cool, tough private eye from an American detective novel of the thirties or forties.

Away from his horn, Young's hip bravado was, if anything, more in evidence. He talked like a never-ending free-verse poem, steeped in colorful metaphor. He had "big eyes" for things he approved of; "no eyes" for things he didn't. He devised nicknames for those closest to him, giving Harry Edison the "Sweets" moniker he would wear all his life and Billie Holiday her "Lady Day" title. Holiday, in turn, said she was the one who inaugurated Young as "president."

Young left the Basie band in 1941 to perform on his own. But neither he nor the band was ever quite the same. He rejoined the band in 1943, but his main concern during these World War II years was trying to avoid the army. He was inducted in 1944 and his fears of what the army had in store for him were confirmed. "He was a man of music now caught in a rigid system of discipline he could not begin to understand," a jazz historian wrote.[5] In 1945, he was tried by a military court for possession of narcotics and sentenced to a year in the detention barracks of Fort Gordon, Georgia.

He was excused from the last few months of his sentence and received a dishonorable discharge. When he got out, he recorded one of his best tunes, "D.B. [for detention barracks] Blues." You can hear the bitterness of the experience in this recording, tempered by a dry, defiant wit and an eagerness to rise above the worst of it. And yet, he never truly got over his ordeal. He described his army experience as "a nightmare, man, one mad nightmare."[6] He played brilliantly off and on from the mid-1940s through the early 1950s. But the sense one gets of Young during these years is of a man battered and bruised by life. During the mid-1950s, he was frequently hospitalized for a variety of ailments, most connected with his alcoholism and depression. He died in March 1959, just three months before Holiday.

By then, Young's quicksilver approach to the tenor saxophone had influenced more than one generation of musicians. Even in the depths of his postwar despair, Young inspired young musicians, who, like millions of listeners, were enthralled by his soft, sensitive sound. Just as singers like Holiday and Ella Fitzgerald were showing how the voice could sound like a jazz instrument, Young proved that an instrument could "sing" jazz with as much humor and sadness as an intimate human voice sharing secrets.

Young's work with Basie inspired his contemporaries to extend their melodic vocabularies while developing new approaches to rhythm. Among the first to exploit such possibilities was another ill-fated improviser named Charlie Christian (1916–1942). Born in Texas and raised in Oklahoma, the guitarist was one of many southwestern jazz musicians scouted by John Hammond, who recommended Christian to Benny Goodman.

Christian's amplified guitar solos with the Goodman group sound more contemporary than the music surrounding him. His taut playing throbs with the kind of out-front virtuosity expected from a horn player more than a guitarist. Like the best music of any era, it seems to belong to no era in particular. Christian also began to play jam sessions at a

Lester Young

Harlem nightclub called Minton's where new ways of playing jazz were being tested. Had he not died of tuberculosis at twenty-seven, Christian might have led the modern jazz movement.

Though Lester Young would continue an off-and-on relationship with Count Basie, the bandleader never found another soloist like "Prez." Still, the band continued to prosper through the 1940s with talents like trombonists Vic Dickenson (1906–1984) and J. J. Johnson (1924–) and saxophonists Buddy Tate (1915–), Illinois Jacquet (1922–), and Don Byas (1912–1972).

The slump in big-band business after World War II eventually caught up with Basie, who in 1949 disbanded his large unit in favor of an octet. In 1952, he reorganized a big band whose power was such that one of its later—and best—albums was called, "The Atomic Mr. Basie." There were featured players like saxophonists Marshall Royal (1912–), Frank Foster (1928–), and Frank Wess (1922–). Singer Joe Williams (1918–) was a little-known blues singer before joining Basie full-time in 1954. Williams's big, smooth vocals helped make him Basie's biggest star since Young.

Some argue that the real stars of the 1950s Basie band were arrangers like Thad Jones (1923–1986) and Neal Hefti (1922–), who wrote such memorable Basie standards as "Little Pony" and "Lil' Darlin.'" Pieces like these kept the Basie band charging hard through the sixties, seventies, and eighties. Under Foster's leadership, it still does.

eight

THE SHOCK OF THE NEW, PART ONE

BY THE EARLY 1940s, many young musicians were made restless by the possibilities for greater individual expression in jazz. They heard virtuosos like Christian, Young, and Tatum create exciting new ways to swing and felt there was room for still more advancement.

One such musician was a nineteen-year-old alto saxophonist from Kansas City who, in 1939, was desperately looking for work in New York. Charlie Parker (1920–1955) had arrived in the Big Apple bedraggled and hungry, looking for a place—any place—to play his horn. He washed dishes in a Harlem hangout where he could hear Art Tatum play the piano. He sat in on jam sessions all over town, absorbing whatever he could learn about harmony and chords. Monroe's, a Harlem nightclub, was where he often went to jam into the night—and learn. As Parker would recall a decade later, it was in December 1939, while practicing the popular tune "Cherokee" in the back room of a chili parlor near Monroe's, that "I came alive."

I'd been getting bored with the stereotyped changes that were being used at the time and I kept thinking there's bound to be something else. I could hear it sometimes, but I couldn't play it. Well, that night I was working on "Cherokee" and as I did I found that by using the higher intervals of a chord as a melody line and backing them with appropriately related changes, I could play the thing I'd been hearing.[1]

Parker wasn't the only one searching for "something else" to do with conventional chord changes and melody lines. At about the same time, a trumpet player named John Birks Gillespie (1917–1993), already better known as "Dizzy," was working with the Cab Calloway big band while cultivating a similar relationship to melody, harmony, and rhythm that Parker was seeking. He pursued these ideas in after-hours jam sessions with a Pittsburgh-born drummer named Kenny Clarke (1914–1985), and a startlingly individualistic pianist named Thelonious Monk (1917–1982).

Each of these and the many people who followed made strong contributions to modern jazz. But it was Parker—bold as Armstrong, creative as Ellington, virtuosic as Tatum, lyrical as Young, and, finally, self-destructive as Holiday—who would be viewed as the central figure in jazz music's mid-century sea change.

There was little—perhaps only a little—in the background of Charles Christopher Parker, Jr., that foretold such magnitude. His father was a sometime singer-pianist on the vaudeville circuit who left the family when Charles, Jr., was nine. His mother, Addie, a nurse, raised him—"spoiled" him is how some older musicians recall it—and encouraged him to play music. She gave him a baritone horn when he was thirteen, but he rejected it in favor of the alto saxophone.

Once Parker got caught up in the Kansas City music scene, he asked questions of every musician he met. The local musicians remembered him as a slow, but intuitive learner. Some also remember Parker being mortified at least twice during jam sessions. Once, while jamming with members of the Count Basie band, drummer Jo Jones became so disgusted with Parker's ignorance of correct chord changes that he lifted his cymbal off its stand and flung it at Parker's feet.

In 1937, Parker, lying about his age, got a professional musician's union card and joined the Kansas City–based band of George E. Lee on a tour of Ozark Mountain resorts. While on the road, he took a bunch of Basie records with him, playing along with Lester Young solos until he'd mastered them. A few months later, Parker was back in Kansas City, a bit more confident, but still ready to learn more. He joined a band led by alto saxophonist Buster Smith, whom Parker had idolized for years.

By this time, Parker was in his late teens, married to the first of four wives, and had a professional reputation. He had also picked up a drug habit that was to plague him for the rest of his brief life. (Later, when Parker was as much an idol to younger musicians as Buster Smith was to him, he agonized over the way these players copied his excessive drug use as much as they did his music.)

In 1938, Parker left Kansas City, first for Chicago and, eventually, to Buster Smith's doorstep in New York, arriving hungry, shabby, legs swollen from having worn his shoes for so long. A year later, he was on the road with a small band when he'd heard his father had been stabbed to death by a jealous woman. He returned to Kansas City and soon joined a band led by blues pianist Jay McShann (1916–).

With McShann's band, Parker began to put everything he'd learned from others together with the discoveries he'd made on his own. Audiences who heard the McShann band in dance halls or on records were startled by the speed, fluidity, and tonal authority of the alto saxophonist who was barely entering his twenties. It was also at about this time that Parker acquired his famous "Yardbird" or "Bird" nickname. Some have traced it to a childhood love

Charlie Parker

for chicken. But at least one account had Parker traveling with McShann and other band members to a Nebraska date when the car they were riding in struck two chickens. McShann remembered Parker saying, "Man, go back, you hit that yardbird." Parker retrieved one of the dead chickens and asked the owner of the house where the band was boarding to cook the bird.[2] By the time Parker returned to New York, everyone seemed to be calling him "Yardbird" or just "Yard," or "Bird."

McShann was proud of his star player. His band brought the alto sax prodigy to the attention of other musicians, notably Dizzy Gillespie, who first heard Parker when the Calloway band stopped in Kansas City. When the two discovered they were working on similar new ideas, a close bond was established, linking them forever in music history.

By this time, Gillespie had been through quite an odyssey of his own, beginning in his Cheraw, South Carolina, birthplace. His father was a bricklayer and part-time bandleader who died when Gillespie was ten. Young John Gillespie began his musical education on the trombone but switched to trumpet at fourteen. He was offered a scholarship to the Laurinburg Institute in North Carolina, where he studied music theory, harmony, and vocational agriculture. In 1935, he dropped out of Laurinburg and followed the rest of his family north to Philadelphia, where he quickly established himself as a jazz musician—and as someone irreverent enough to be called "Dizzy." ("The guys started calling me that in '35 in Philly, as indicative of my impetuous youth," he later said.)[3.]

Gillespie worshiped Roy Eldridge's big, sky-scraping sound. Someday, Gillespie would demonstrate that he could not only play as high and as hard as Eldridge, but at a faster tempo.

In 1937, Gillespie was hired by bandleader-saxophonist Teddy Hill. Hill disbanded his unit in 1940, but his relationship with Gillespie was extended at Minton's. It was at this legendary spot that Gillespie, Clarke, Monk, Christian, and older musicians like Fats Waller and Lester Young took part in late-night jam sessions. Minton's and Monroe's, through the World War II years, were regarded as incubators of the modern sound. The pace was fierce and demanding at both clubs. Often, at Minton's, the house band of Monk, Clarke, and bassist Nick Fenton threw in complicated chord patterns or breakneck rhythms just to see who, among the newcomers, could keep up.

Gillespie had meanwhile been hired by Cab Calloway (1907–1994), a popular song-and-dance man best known for the comic dirge "Minnie the Moocher." Gillespie's employment with Calloway was a fitful one. Once, when the trumpeter let fly with an especially complex solo, Calloway responded peevishly. "I don't want you playing that [expletive] music in my band," he told Gillespie.[4]

Calloway's reaction typified the attitudes of many older jazz musicians. Although Louis Armstrong came to respect the artistry of Gillespie and others in the modern movement, he never embraced their innovations, which was ironic, since it was Armstrong's own improvisational daring that led to later experiments.

Gillespie's employment with Calloway took him all over the country, where he met other young innovators like Parker, and a Minneapolis bassist named Oscar Pettiford (1922–1960), whose propulsive playing was strongly reminiscent of Jimmy Blanton's. (Indeed, he would play three years with Blanton's employer, Duke Ellington.) Gillespie encouraged these players to go to New York and work with some of the other creative musicians stretching their ideas at Minton's and Monroe's.

A wartime ban on recording imposed by the musicians' union between 1942 and 1944 has perpetuated the mystique of those after-hours sessions at Minton's and Monroe's where, witnesses have reported, the musical

Cab Calloway

ferment was exciting, especially when Parker and Gillespie were around. By then, both men had left their respective breakthrough band gigs. Parker quietly left the McShann band in 1941. Gillespie's departure from the Calloway band that same year was more dramatic. A spitball hit the back of the leader's neck during a performance at Hartford's State Theater. Backstage, Calloway accused Gillespie (mistakenly, it turned out) of shooting the paper ball. The two men got into a violent argument. Calloway swiped at Gillespie, who retaliated with a knife. Neither man was seriously injured, but Gillespie was told to walk.

Eventually, Parker and Gillespie were recruited for pianist Earl Hines's big band. Because of the ban, no recordings exist of the band in this eight-month period between 1942 and 1943. But it was considered one of the most innovative units of the era, having Gillespie and Parker along with two vocalists who achieved great fame in the postwar era: Billy Eckstine (1914–1993) and Sarah Vaughan (1924–1990).

Eckstine, a dashing baritone, left Hines to form his own big band in 1944. Gillespie, Parker, and Vaughan signed on, as did such future stars as tenor saxophonists Wardell Gray (1921–1955), Dexter Gordon (1923– 1989), and Gene Ammons (1925–1974), and drummer Art Blakey (1919–1990). In fact, for much of the 1940s, Eckstine's band employed some of the most significant players in modern jazz.

The experience with Hines's band put the finishing touches on Gillespie's and Parker's apprenticeship. Both were gaining a small, but rapidly growing following through appearances in clubs up and down Manhattan's 52nd Street, which was becoming so famous for its abundance of nightclubs that music fans referred to it simply as "The Street." And the music being developed in its clubs was becoming known as "bebop" or "bop."

Whatever the music was called, it was drastically different from anything that came before, beginning with the rhythms. Before bebop, each of the two or four beats in every jazz tune's bar (or measure) was stressed by a bass drum. At the late-night jams at Minton's, Kenny Clarke experimented with shifting the beat's emphasis to the top cymbal of a drum set. Clarke's style was picked up by another young drummer who often played with Parker at Monroe's jam sessions. Brooklyn-born Max Roach (1925–) soon mastered the new rhythmic approach to the point where he could make it do anything he wanted.

Gillespie's high-altitude, high-speed playing was as breathtaking on ballads like "I Can't Get Started," as it was on such Gillespie compositions as "A Night in Tunisia." To his performances, he also brought a comic persona that tickled audiences. One of his most enduring bandstand gags began with his telling the audience, "And now we'd like to introduce the members of the band." He and the other musicians would then exchange greetings and hand-shakes with each other.

Parker's appeal came from the torrent of ideas and emotions surging from his saxophone. "Parker spoke through his horn," critic Leonard Feather wrote, "like a consumer of basic English who had suddenly swallowed the whole dictionary yet miraculously managed to digest every page."[5]

Parker's mastery of chord changes in both blues and pop tunes had, by the early forties, reached a level where he could rapidly invent and reinvent phrases. Parker invented whole new melodies on those chord changes that became as familiar as the songs they were based on. The chord changes of "Cherokee," for example, were the foundation for "Ko-Ko," which Gillespie and Parker recorded in 1945. And if you listen closely to Parker's "Moose the Mooche," you can identify the chord changes to George Gershwin's "I Got Rhythm."

One tune Parker played at a Los Angeles recording session in 1946 was Gillespie's "A Night in Tunisia." At one point he recorded a four-bar break of such breathtaking ingenuity and force that all those in the studio were shaken—including the rhythm section, which stumbled so badly that another take was required.

In July of that year, Parker suffered a nervous breakdown as a result of heroin addiction. He was confined for six months in the Camarillo State Hospital in California. He emerged in the winter of 1947, refreshed, restored, his demons at bay—for the time being. The robust tune he recorded soon after his release, "Relaxin' at Camarillo," typified his mood and work for the next few years.

Parker's mystique, combined with Gillespie's flair for showmanship and public relations, helped bring bebop to jazz's forefront. Soon, other young musicians, along with older ones like Hawkins and Young, were getting into the modern groove. The younger musicians were becoming almost as celebrated as Parker—and just as star-crossed.

The principal pianist of the bebop era, for instance, was the brilliant and troubled Earl "Bud" Powell (1924–1966), who used the same dynamic attack on his instrument that Gillespie and Parker deployed on theirs. He had much of Art Tatum's stylistic power, braced by a facility with rhythm and harmony that brought drama and haunting beauty to his performances. Powell's career was an erratic one, interrupted by bouts with mental illness and alcoholism. Through it all, he created a legacy that was both influential and singular among pianists who followed his lead.

Some of Powell's more memorable recordings, aside from those within a trio or solo setting, were with Theodore "Fats" Navarro (1923–1950), a Florida-born trumpeter who had taken Gillespie's place in the Billy Eckstine orchestra and brought a fiery lyricism to Gillespie's rapid-fire attack. "They called him 'Fat Girl,'" recalled singer Carmen McRae, "because he was sort of a cherub, big fat jaws and a big stomach. . . . [He played] the most beautiful horn, forever practicing, forever striving."[6] Sadly, Navarro's health was weakened by heroin use and he died of tuberculosis before he could further develop his brilliant style.

Other musicians were bringing their instruments up to speed for the modern era. Tenor saxophonists Dexter Gordon and Wardell Gray engaged in spirited horn duels that galvanized audiences in New York and Los Angeles.

The slide trombone seemed the least likely instrument to adapt to bebop's new melodic and rhythmic challenges. But J. J. Johnson (1924–) gave this seemingly unwieldy horn the same agility of tone and phrasing that Parker, Gillespie, and the others poured through their instruments. The same could be said for Sarah Vaughan. A soprano with the range of an opera diva, Vaughan had a way of inventing within a given melody or phrase that matched the creativity of bebopping instrumentalists.

Toward the end of the 1940s, the bebop movement had all but galvanized the jazz mainstream. So much so that the small combo—the main form for conveying the new sounds—all but surpassed the big band as a major force in the music. Some bands rode the changes by engaging in the same kind of formal experimentation that led to bebop.

Among the bands that best absorbed the innovative spirit was a popular unit led by clarinetist Woody Herman (1913–1987), who called his bands "thundering herds" or "herds" for short. The name was appropriate. Herman's bands were roaring, rambunctious groups infused with the energy, wit, and flair for invention of an elite bop quintet. The herds' crown jewel was its crack saxophone section which, between 1947 and 1949, featured tenors Zoot Sims, Stan Getz, and Al Cohn, and baritone Serge Chaloff, known as the "Four Brothers." Sims, Cohn, and Getz figured prominently in the music's future. But Chaloff (1923–1957) deserves a larger place in jazz history than he's received for bestowing bop wings to his large, deep-voiced horn.

The most furiously innovative big band of the era was led by Dizzy Gillespie himself. He first tried to organize an orchestra in 1945, but the group didn't last the year. He tried again in 1946, and the results were as startling and as initially controversial as his first small-group recordings with Parker. The tempos were quick, the arrangements complex. The horn sections were extensions of Gillespie's own approach to the trumpet. In the next few years, as the band toured the country, they faced hostility from audiences who weren't expecting a band geared more for listening than dancing. But, even with its rough edges (or, more likely because of them), there was an excitement in this orchestrated bebop that still comes through in recordings from the period.

The most significant innovation of Gillespie's big band was its introduction of Caribbean rhythms to the jazz idiom. Between 1947 and 1948, the band enjoyed the services of African-Cuban percussionist Luciano Gonzales, who performed under the name Chano Pozo (1915–1948). In December 1947, the band recorded three of the best-known examples of the jazz-Afro-Cuban fusion: "Cubano Be," "Cubano Bop," and "Manteca." Pozo's chantlike singing and conga-drum playing on these tunes sounded both very new and very old, harking back to black music's ancestral roots. A year after these sessions, Pozo was shot and killed in an East Harlem bar fight.

By 1950, Gillespie, like other big-band leaders, would be forced by economic necessity to disband his orchestra. Yet its legacy would stretch well into the following decade. Gillespie also continued to play, off and on, with the man he would call "the other side of my heartbeat," Charlie Parker.

Between 1947 and 1948, Parker led a quintet regarded as the music's cutting-edge combo. Along with Parker, the members were drummer Max Roach, pianist Duke Jordan (sometimes Al Haig), bassist Tommy Potter, and trumpeter Miles Davis (1926–1992), who had spent some time at the prestigious Juilliard School of Music before dropping out to continue his education on The Street. More—

Dizzy Gillespie

much more—would be heard from Davis in the following decades.

Parker's music continued to grow in influence. He made a series of records with string sections that, while derided for slickness even today, nonetheless feature some of his most beautiful playing. For all his great innovations, Parker remained, at heart, a Kansas City blues man. He seems relaxed and in command when playing "K.C. Blues" or "Parker's Mood," a 1948 blues piece which, though invented on the spot, seems as logically conceived as a written composition.

When hearing "Parker's Mood," it's not hard to feel both the vitality and the melancholy that seemed constantly at odds in Parker's soul. Such conflict may have been the root of the emotional turbulence that plagued his final years. The death of a two-year-old daughter in 1953 pitched him into an emotional tailspin from which he never recovered. His drug use worsened and so did his health. When Parker died in March 1955, a doctor had estimated his age to be somewhere in his fifties or sixties. In fact, he was only thirty-four.

Parker's posthumous cult first took shape in subway graffiti that proclaimed, "Bird Lives!" With each passing year, it's becoming clear that Parker *does* live, in recordings that, almost fifty years after they were made, amaze first-, second- or hundredth-time listeners. His life may have been a mess—and he was the first to tell his idolaters to "do as I say, not as I do." But his art continues to tell all who listen that you can take chances, make something new out of the old and take hold of whatever your imagination insists can be done.

"They teach you there's a boundary line to music," Parker once said, "but man, there's no boundary line to art."[7] Musicians aren't the only ones who have taken heart from this message.

nine

PLAYING THE CHANGES

BEBOP, with its frenzied inventiveness, was appropriate background music for America in the late 1940s, a time of atomic bombs, supersonic jets, and fast-paced economic growth.

But bebop wasn't the only African-American music taking flight in the years following World War II. "Rhythm and blues" (R&B) was a catchall name for a rousing mix of blues and dance music that, wrote one historian, "embodied the fervor of gospel music, the throbbing vigor of boogie-woogie, the jump beat of swing and the gutsiness and sexuality of life in the Black ghetto."[1]

One of R&B's first stars was alto saxophonist Louis Jordan (1908–1975), who apprenticed in vaudeville and with Chick Webb's orchestra before forming his own group in the late 1930s. Throughout the 1940s, Jordan and his combo mixed spicy African-American street repartee with gritty, brassy blues arrangements to fashion such popular tunes as "Choo-Choo Ch'Boogie," "Caledonia," and "Let the Good Times Roll."

Many influential blues voices emerged in the postwar years. Guitarist Aaron "T-Bone" Walker (1910–1975) came out of Texas with a big, electrically amplified sound delivered with a powerful rhythmic drive. John Lee Hooker (1917–) and McKinley Morganfield (1915–1987), better known as Muddy Waters, carried the Mississippi Delta blues legacy of Robert Johnson roaring and kicking into the new era.

There were also popular African-American musicians who seemed to belong to no movement or genre except the one established by their own popularity. Pianist Erroll Garner (1926–1977), who learned his craft entirely by ear, enjoyed fame and fortune from the mid-1940s through the 1960s. When he played tunes like his famed "Frankie and Johnny Fantasy" from the forties, or his phenomenally popular fifties ballad, "Misty," Garner brought an engaging big-band sound to the piano.

Another pianist, Nat "King" Cole (1919–1965), enjoyed a combination of public renown and artistic respect of a magnitude that only Louis Armstrong before him—and practically no jazz musicians since—could claim. His playing put him near the front rank of jazz pianists. But it was his velvety singing that made him a superstar.

Cole's piano playing and singing gained widespread attention in the mid-1940s with a drumless trio that discharged hit ("Straighten Up and Fly Right") after hit ("Route 66"), after hit ("Hit That Jive, Jack"). As a vocalist, Cole influenced such rhythm-and-blues stars as Charles Brown (1920–), and a blind Atlanta pianist named Ray Charles (1930–), whose searing vocals and boundary-breaching musical intelligence would, by the mid-1950s, bring gospel-inflected dynamism to blues, pop, country-western, and jazz music.

Bebop and rhythm and blues brought forth an age of modernism in African-American music. The country's music scene rapidly grew in scope and diversity as it headed toward the early 1950s. Bebop was at the cutting edge of this transition. But swing music also retained a large follow-

Nat "King" Cole

ing despite the decline of big bands. Classic New Orleans jazz also found new audiences during the late 1940s.

Yet within modern jazz itself, there were stirrings of a movement that would constitute a reaction against—and an extension of—many of the ideas advanced by the beboppers. The two musicians who best embodied this trend were Thelonious Monk and Miles Davis. Both had been active participants in the bop upheaval: Monk in his legendary early forties stint as Minton's house pianist, Davis in his stormy late forties tenure with Charlie Parker's quintet.

While those in the advance guard of bebop sought to overrun the empty spaces between phrases with still more phrases, Davis and Monk made dramatic use of those spaces. Both promoted a "less-is-more" approach to modern jazz.

Davis's trumpet playing was lighter and cooler than Fats Navarro's or Dizzy Gillespie's. His spare, melodic attack, in fact, seemed to reach back over the heads of the modernists to the swing era. Always in Davis's playing there was a subtle passion expressed plaintively in a manner more reminiscent of Billie Holiday and Lester Young than of any trumpet-playing contemporary.

Miles Dewey Davis was born in Alton, Illinois, a suburb of East St. Louis. His father was a prominent dentist and prosperous farmer. Davis grew up confident, fiercely proud of his blackness. His father gave him a trumpet for his thirteenth birthday. Miles played the trumpet in his high school band and began hanging out with area musicians, notably trumpeter Clark Terry, who was an early influence. His father came up with the idea of sending Miles to Juilliard—but the New York jazz scene exerted a stronger pull.

Davis played with Coleman Hawkins and with the Billy Eckstine band before joining Parker's combo in 1947. Davis's star rose with the leader's. But the trumpeter was becoming irritated with his boss's erratic behavior. Often he had to lead the quintet in Parker's place when the altoist was late or absent. He split with Parker in December, 1948. By then, Davis had also been working with nine musicians who played jazz that was smoother and leaner than what bebop fans were accustomed to. The music was arranged by two members of the "experimental" Claude Thornhill band: pianist Gil Evans (1912–1988) and baritone saxophonist Gerry Mulligan (1927–). The nonet's instrumentation was unusual. A French horn and a tuba were matched with Davis's trumpet and a trombone played by either J. J. Johnson or Kai Winding.

Along with Mulligan, the only other saxophone was an alto played by Lee Konitz (1927–), another Thornhill band member, who was also making his name playing in a small experimental combo led by pianist Lennie Tristano (1919–1978).

In January 1949, Davis, Konitz, Mulligan, and the rest of the nonet recorded what became known as the "Birth of the Cool" sessions, named for the album later released, to great success, compiling these sessions. Davis began to acquire a reputation independent of Parker and the bebop movement. But his advancement in the early 1950s was hindered by a bout with heroin addiction he would overcome, on his own, in four years' time. During those years— 1951 through 1955—he recorded, despite his troubles, some quirky, lyrical music with such young, emerging players as alto saxophonist Jackie McLean (1932–) and tenor saxophonist Sonny Rollins (1930–). He also worked with more-established players like J. J. Johnson, Max Roach, and, in a memorable 1954 session, Thelonious Monk.

Like Davis, Monk found himself, by the late forties, on the outside of bebop looking in. He was regarded in those years as an oddity, even by his fellow musicians. Born in North Carolina, Monk was raised in New York and felt his way around the piano from the age of six until he started

formal training by age eleven. In three years, he was playing at Harlem parties and learning from such masters of
stride piano as James P. Johnson.

Another influence was Mary Lou Williams, who had
first heard the teenaged Monk in the mid-1930s, when he
toured through Kansas City with an evangelical road show.
Williams later recalled that Monk's approach to melody
and rhythm was fully formed by their first encounter.

At Minton's, Monk's unconventional chord combina-
tions were attracting attention from the musicians who
played there. It was also at about this time—1939–
1940—that Monk wrote and performed many of the tunes
that were to become jazz standards: "Ruby My Dear,"
"Epistrophy," "Round Midnight," "Well, You Needn't,"
"Rhythm-a-ning."

Only Gillespie and Parker were in Monk's company as
1940s innovators. Yet Bird and Dizzy reaped acclaim
through the decade, while Monk was considered at best an
obscure, marginal figure. At worst, he was ridiculed as
"weird." Coleman Hawkins, one of Monk's earliest advo-
cates, would hear such complaints when Monk played in
his combo in 1944 at various 52nd Street clubs.

Through this difficult period, Monk stuck to his artistic
guns. He was given a chance to record under his own
name in 1947 for Blue Note. The music challenged musicians who played with Monk on the sessions over the next
five years. "You really had to have ears to play with him,"
recalled Blue Note recording director, Alfred Lion.[2]

Yet it's clear, especially in hindsight, that there was
something both old *and* new about the music on these early
recordings. Monk's relationship to rhythm may have sounded odd, but his *sense* of rhythm was reminiscent of an old-
fashioned ragtime or stride performance by James P.
Johnson or Fats Waller. Tunes like "Straight No Chaser" and
"Misterioso" were quirky, spare, and—the more one listened to them—great fun.

For example, "Evidence," recorded in 1948, was based on the chord changes in the pop tune "Just You, Just Me." Monk states the melody by firing one chord into each measure. Each shot is in sync with the song's harmony. Through such compositions, Monk proved that the *form* of a jazz piece could assert the musician's personality as much as the improvisations within it.

These recordings sold well among jazz fans. But Monk still bewildered mainstream listeners, even those who had become comfortable with bebop. Worse, in 1951, he was arrested and imprisoned on a narcotics charge (which many witnesses of the time believe was false). He was barred from playing in New York nightclubs for several years.

It was interesting—and appropriate—that the fortunes of both Davis and Monk began to change at about the same time. There was tension between the two men on a recording session in December 1954. Davis asked Monk not to play behind him for two of the three pieces being recorded that Christmas Eve. ("The reason I told Monk to lay out," Davis later recalled in his autobiography, "was because Monk never did know how to play behind a horn player . . . especially trumpet players.")[3] Yet these two masters of time and space were at their best on that session.

The following year, Davis returned to prominence with a performance at the Newport Jazz Festival of Monk's "Round Midnight." Monk, meanwhile, had been signed to a recording contract that, for the rest of the decade, yielded some of the best music of its time. Although it would be another decade before his fame caught up to Davis's, Monk was now an inspiration for other jazz musicians. Davis's description of Monk's influence is characteristically succinct: "[It] has to do with giving musicians more freedom. They feel that if Monk can do what he does, they can. Monk has been using space for a long time."[4]

The same would be said of Davis, who, in 1955, had

formed the first in a series of influential small groups he led to international stardom. Drummer Philly Joe Jones (1923–1985) and bassist Paul Chambers (1935–1969) anchored the group. The soft, graceful playing of pianist Red Garland (1923–1984) added to the melodic decor.

And there was a little-known tenor saxophonist who was still trying to find a clear direction for his dense, torrential style. John Coltrane (1926–1967) provided as perfect a complement to Davis's spare playing as Davis did for Parker. But Coltrane, in those years, had an appetite for drink and drugs. Coltrane's erratic behavior prompted Davis to fire him from the quintet in the spring of 1957.

The tenor saxophonist spent the summer cleaning up his act and playing in a quartet that, both at recording sessions and in an electrifying engagement at New York's Five Spot club, would lead Coltrane to greater command of his music. The group's leader was Thelonious Monk.

Davis's other significant work in the late 1950s was with Gil Evans, with whom he'd worked nearly a decade earlier on the "Birth of the Cool" sessions. Evans used a large orchestra to frame Davis's introspective solos on three of the best jazz orchestra albums of the postbebop era: "Miles Ahead" (1957), "Porgy and Bess" (1958), and "Sketches of Spain" (1959).

By the time Davis and Evans renewed their professional association, the "cool jazz" movement they had helped forge was solidly planted in a thriving jazz marketplace. When "cool jazz" began its rise at the start of the 1950s, its smooth texture, light tone, and minimal design were seen as a response to the frenetic, heated pace of bebop. But it also extended bop ideas and enhanced the values of swing, especially those exemplified by Lester Young.

Young's influence was especially apparent in the playing of Stan Getz (1927–1991), who may have been the biggest of bandleader Woody Herman's tenor sax stars. He left Herman's band in 1949 and found even greater renown leading small combos. Getz was nicknamed "The

Miles Davis

Sound." But his warm, soft tone and flair for melody entitled him to share the nickname Frank Sinatra was given early in his career: "The Voice."

From its "birth," cool jazz stressed intimate surroundings, technical skill, and a delicate balance of melancholy and dry wit. Gerry Mulligan embodied all these values in his baritone sax playing and his pianoless quartets, the first of which, formed in 1952, made stars out of percussionist Chico Hamilton (1921–) and trumpeter Chet Baker (1929–1988).

Partly because the Mulligan-Baker group first recorded in Los Angeles, the "cool" sound seemed tied to the West Coast. Thus, "West Coast sound" became synonymous with "cool jazz." The term was misleading since many L.A.-based players, like Dexter Gordon, saxophonist Art Pepper (1925–1982), pianist Hampton Hawes (1928–1977), and, especially, bassist-composer Charles Mingus (1922–1979), tended to be anything but "cool" in their approaches to jazz.

Yet "California" and "cool" remained linked—especially after the emergence, in the mid-1950s, of a pair of California natives named Dave Brubeck (1920–) and Paul Desmond (1924–1977). Pianist Brubeck and saxophonist Desmond formed an alliance that, in various small groups through the 1950s and 1960s, would prove as popular as the Mulligan-Baker connection.

The most challenging of the cool modernists was Lennie Tristano, who adapted much of the complexity in Parker's innovations while scaling down its tempestuous energy. Tristano's horn players, like Lee Konitz and tenor saxophonist Warne Marsh (1927–1987), contributed to an image of Tristano's music as so cool that it was glacial.

The same description has been applied to the Modern Jazz Quartet, which was formed in 1952. Pianist John Lewis (1920–) was founder and leader of the group, which, at the start, included bassist Percy Heath (1923–), vibraphonist Milt Jackson (1923–), and drummer Kenny

Clarke. The only personnel change in more than four decades of the MJQ's existence was Clarke's replacement in 1955 by Connie Kay (1927–1994).

Like Davis, Monk, and the cool-schoolers, Lewis and his group preferred to say more with the fewest effects. The beat was kept at a pace that rarely rose above a gentle throb. Many of their pieces leaned heavily on counterpoint, polyphony, and other formal elements. Yet for all its classical elements, the group has a firm command of blues and swing. They disbanded in 1974, but reorganized in 1981. Since then, the MJQ has played with greater brio and vitality as it cruises toward its fifth decade.

As "cool jazz" was pleasing listeners, "hard bop," another extension of bebop's ideas, was also attracting devotees. This music differed from "cool jazz" because it emphasized thicker harmonies, a heavier beat, and an abundance of themes, melodies, and riffs derived from blues and gospel music.

Much of the music Miles Davis played in the early to mid-1950s shared these qualities, especially in the 1954 tune "Walkin'." Among those playing with Davis on that classic blues was pianist Horace Silver (1928–), who, by the late fifties, was regarded as the quintessential hard-bop composer-musician. Discovered in 1950 by Stan Getz, Silver worked with the tenor saxophonist for a year before striking out on his own as one of New York's busiest session players.

The same year as Davis's "Walkin'" session, Silver organized a quintet featuring trumpeter Kenny Dorham (1924–1977), tenor saxophonist Hank Mobley (1930–1986), bassist Doug Watkins (1934–1962), and drummer Art Blakey (1919–1990). The group recorded under a name, "Jazz Messengers," that Blakey had used for a larger ensemble he'd led several years earlier.

Blakey was the most experienced member of this group, having worked with such bandleaders as Fletcher Henderson, Mary Lou Williams, and Billy Eckstine before

Thelonious Monk

leaving for Africa in 1947 for a brief stay. He returned to America a more confident player, with a compelling, thunderous style distinguished by furious press rolls, double-tempo speed runs, and rattling rim shots. He was one of the first drummers to catch on to what Thelonious Monk was up to, and played with the pianist on his ground-breaking recordings in the late 1940s.

The 1954 Messengers' recording, released under Silver's name, included two of the pianist's compositions, "Doodlin'" and "The Preacher," that would characterize the hard-bop sound. Both had a driving beat and simple melody that owed as much to rhythm-and-blues as to bebop. The mix of blues and gospel elements was so strong that this strain of jazz was called "funk" or "soul" jazz.

By 1956, Silver was recording and performing on his own. "Sister Sadie," "Blowin' the Blues Away," "The Cape Verdean Blues," and "Song for My Father" are just a few of Silver's pieces that have become gilt-edged jazz standards.

The success of "funk" jazz in the late fifties also spurred the rapid rise of organist Jimmy Smith (1925–), who brought to the Hammond organ the same rhythmic agility and lyrical range that Coleman Hawkins and Charlie Parker introduced to their saxes.

Blakey meanwhile became sole leader of the Jazz Messengers in 1956. Over the next four decades, the band's membership turned over again and again. Under Blakey's demanding, energetic leadership, the Messengers served as a training academy for some of the best and brightest jazz musicians of the modern era.

Among those who have served Blakey's hard-bop cause with distinction: pianists Bobby Timmons, Cedar Walton, Keith Jarrett, Joanne Brackeen, Chick Corea, James Williams, and Geoff Keezer; saxophonists Jackie McLean, Johnny Griffin, Benny Golson, Wayne Shorter, Bobby Watson, and Branford Marsalis; trumpeters Bill Hardman, Lee Morgan, Freddie Hubbard, Chuck Mangione, Woody

Shaw, Randy Brecker, Wynton Marsalis, and Terence Blanchard. Not all continued to march under the hard-bop banner. But Blakey insisted they leave his ranks able to lead and write as well as they played. As one prominent alumnus put it, "Art creates leaders."

Many of the trumpeters who worked with Blakey over the years, especially Morgan, Hubbard, and Shaw, carried on the legacy of one of the greatest virtuosos of the 1950s. Clifford Brown (1930–1956) was regarded as a hero by the jazz community. And it wasn't only because of his bright tone and dazzling technique. Musicians admired "Brownie" for his affability. He seemed free of the drugs and personal demons that had caused so many other musicians of the era to self-destruct. Brown was also a whiz at chess and mathematics. His intelligence, discipline, and talent made him seem destined for great things.

In just four short years prior to his death, at twenty-five, in a car accident, Brown established himself as one of the most dynamic players in jazz history. He could play at any speed with clarity, boldness, and warmth. He began his professional career playing with a rhythm-and-blues group before joining Tadd Dameron's band in 1953. He toured Europe with Lionel Hampton's orchestra and returned to play with various small groups.

In 1954, he joined Max Roach's small combo and the drummer was so impressed with his new trumpeter that he made Brown a co-leader. Over the next few years, the Brown-Roach quintet made some of the most vital records of the decade. Brown's ample melodic resources broadened under Roach's influence. Roach, in turn, seemed inspired by Brown's daring to expand his pursuit of the drum set's expressive possibilities.

Among those who played with Brown and Roach on their last sessions was tenor saxophonist Sonny Rollins, who, along with Getz and Coltrane, was one of the major players on his instrument during the 1950s—and, along with

Brown, a potent virtuoso of a decade rich with jazz talent. As a boy, Theodore Walter Rollins had fallen in love with the bright light reflecting off a golden alto saxophone lying in an open case. His fondness for Louis Jordan also sealed his desire to play the alto, though he switched to the tenor later on. His interest was fueled by some of the people living in his Harlem neighborhood, including Coleman Hawkins and Thelonious Monk. He often rehearsed with Monk in his apartment, absorbing the pianist's intricate use of harmony and rhythm.

In 1951, the young tenor began recording with Miles Davis and soon after began making his own records as a leader. His voice took shape in the early 1950s: a taut, vinegary tone with some of Hawkins's power, some of Young's grace, and an imaginative energy all his own. He had also become so physically imposing that he was called "Newk," for his resemblance to Don Newcombe, a large Brooklyn Dodgers pitching star of the 1950s.

By the mid-1950s, Rollins had worked with just about every important jazz musician of the decade, including Brown, Coltrane, Roach, Blakey, Monk, Silver, and the Modern Jazz Quartet. He was becoming such a commanding force on his instrument that he was called "Saxophone Colossus," which happened to be the title of his 1956 album, one of the greatest ever made.

At various times in his long and distinguished career, Rollins has chosen suddenly to drop out of recording and performing for a few years. The first time was in 1954. The second came four years after the "Colossus" triumph. From 1959 to 1961, the only way one could hear Rollins play was at night on the Williamsburg Bridge linking Manhattan and Brooklyn. He practiced until he believed he was ready to return to the jazz scene. He recorded an album, "The Bridge," that paid tribute to his period of growth and renewal. He continued to play and record until 1968, when he spent five months in India on a spiritual quest. He

Sonny Rollins

then withdrew from music from 1969 to 1971. From 1972 onward, he's been playing with the same invigorating capacity for surprise that he displayed four decades earlier.

When surveying the landscape of jazz history, the late 1950s appears especially lush and fruitful. The big bands of Duke Ellington and Count Basie had gotten a glorious second wind. Both hard bop and cool jazz were holding their own with record buyers, even while the rock-and-roll phenomenon was gathering steam. Thelonious Monk was slowly emerging from the margins of cult renown to widespread respect for his innovations. Dizzy Gillespie was drawing energy from a new big band even more powerful than the one that startled people in the late forties. Louis Armstrong was taking so many goodwill tours throughout the world that he became "Ambassador Satch."

Older stars like Coleman Hawkins and his onetime Fletcher Henderson bandmate, trumpeter Henry "Red" Allen (1908–1967), were drawing renewed attention for their artistry. And there were newer stars breaking out toward decade's end, notably guitarist Wes Montgomery (1925–1968), a self-taught player whose thick chords, big-octave sound and sure-handed sense of swing would carry him to great popularity in the 1960s.

Two pianists with dramatically different styles also flourished in these years. Canadian-born Oscar Peterson (1925–) emerged in the early 1950s with the most startling technical proficiency since Art Tatum. Peterson also had Erroll Garner's ability to make his piano sound like a full-blown orchestra. All this, combined with a facility with swing, assured Peterson steady, widespread success.

Another pianist, more introspective than Peterson, had a profound effect on succeeding generations. Bill Evans (1929–1980) was hired by Miles Davis in 1958 to play in what had become a sextet featuring John Coltrane, Paul Chambers, drummer Jimmy Cobb (1929–), and a bright young alto sax player from Florida named Julian Adderley

(1928–1975), whose big frame and jovial nature won him the name "Cannonball."

Evans's restrained playing was a quality Davis admired. "The sound he got," Davis later said, "was like crystal notes or sparkling water cascading from some clear waterfall."[4]

Pianist Cecil Taylor (1930–) wasn't as famous as Evans or Peterson. Yet when he emerged in the mid-1950s, he was recognized by critics for playing "way outside" conventional jazz music. ("Outside" or "way out" were other names used for the kind of adventurous music Taylor pioneered.) Trained in such classical schools as the New England Conservatory of Music, Taylor has claimed influences ranging from modern European masters such as Igor Stravinsky and Béla Bartók, to a broad array of jazz pianists such as Fats Waller, Horace Silver, Erroll Garner, Lennie Tristano, Dave Brubeck, and Bud Powell.

Of those who were experimenting throughout the fifties outside mainstream jazz, the figure of Charles Mingus (1922–1979) looms largest. A moody, volatile bassist-composer, Mingus expanded thematic and rhythmic possibilities for jazz performance and composition as significantly as had Ellington and Monk. Yet, it has taken some time for his importance to be recognized.

Born in Nogales, Arizona, Mingus grew up in the Watts section of Los Angeles. He came to love music in the church services he attended with his stepmother. He first heard Ellington's music on the radio when he was eight or nine years old. He studied trombone, piano, and cello before choosing the bass as his main instrument. During the early 1940s, Mingus was becoming a West Coast legend for his virtuoso bass playing. He spent a brief period touring with Louis Armstrong's orchestra before returning to L.A. to lead several ensembles under the name "Baron" Mingus.

Mingus had coronated himself "Baron" in tribute to his

idol, Ellington. Charlie Parker soon became another one of Mingus's heroes after the bassist saw him at various West Coast clubs. (Indeed, in 1953, Mingus played the bass behind Parker, Gillespie, Max Roach, and Bud Powell at a show in Toronto's Massey Hall that some call the greatest jazz concert ever.)

In 1947, Mingus joined the Lionel Hampton band and drew his first whiff of nationwide exposure with a tune he'd written for Hampton called "Mingus Fingers." He became even more famous while employed by another vibraphonist, Red Norvo (1908–), who added Mingus to a trio that included guitarist Tal Farlow (1921–). The trio's recordings between 1950 and 1951 were acclaimed by critics and listeners. They also helped solidify Mingus's credentials as a jazz modernist.

Mingus moved to New York and got busy. He worked with such stars as Powell and Lennie Tristano. With Max Roach, he set up an independent, short-lived record company, Debut, and joined a group of experimental musicians and composers. He gradually collected a core group of musicians sympathetic to his grand designs.

In 1956, he recorded the album "Pithecanthropus Erectus." The title track tells the story of the attempt of an early hominid to walk on two legs. This watershed work, a prelude to much of the free-flowing jazz of the next decade, is typical of Mingus's best work: harmonic density, thematic grandeur, and a dramatic sense of form able to contain abrupt shifts in tempo, tone, and mood.

Mingus's late-fifties work was also marked by social protest. "Fables of Faubus," written in 1959, took its name from the governor of Arkansas who, two years earlier, had used National Guard troops to prevent black children from entering a Little Rock high school. (This was the same incident that aroused Louis Armstrong's public scorn.)

The variety of Mingus's work is impressive, ranging from the intensity of "Haitian Fight Song," "Wednesday

Charles Mingus

Night Prayer Meeting," and "Better Get Hit in Your Soul," to the tenderness of "Eclipse," "Self Portrait in Three Colors," and "Goodbye Pork Pie Hat," a tribute to Lester Young.

By the early sixties, the innovations pioneered by Mingus were being carried through by many musicians and embraced by listeners and critics. Yet toward mid-decade, Mingus was in a state of emotional exhaustion due to financial and psychological troubles. He spent the late 1960s away from music, working on his autobiography, *Beneath the Underdog*. After its publication in 1971, he returned to active performing and recording. He continued to nurture musicians and acquired greater recognition of his accomplishments as a player, leader, and composer. After being diagnosed in 1977 with "Lou Gehrig's disease" (amyotrophic lateral sclerosis), a degenerative disease affecting the spinal cord and resulting in increasing muscular weakness, he continued to direct musicians from a wheelchair.

Mingus, who was fond of mysticism, was convinced that his music wouldn't receive respect during his lifetime. His widow, Susan, recalls that Mingus believed he would someday return in another life as a cellist in a symphony orchestra playing the work of Charles Mingus.

ten

THE SHOCK OF THE NEW, PART TWO

FOR JAZZ, the 1960s—an era of upheaval and transition throughout the world—started a year before the decade got under way. Two recording sessions took place early in 1959 that would define the music's course for the next several years.

Before these sessions, the norm in jazz had been to "play the changes": in other words, to build improvisations on the chords of whatever song the musicians were playing. Artists like Charles Mingus and Cecil Taylor were, in their distinctive ways, challenging this orthodoxy. Monk, like Mingus, continued to explore different approaches to melody and rhythm. Improvisers were inspired to greater creativity by Sonny Rollins's example.

But, as he often would in the next several years, Miles Davis charted the next course for jazz musicians to follow. In March 1959, members of Davis's sextet assembled for a recording session unlike any other. The leader came in with only a few sketches of what he wanted. These pieces encouraged a *modal* rather than a harmonic strategy for improvisation. In other words, the musicians' improvisations would take off from the notes of a scale rather than from chords.

To this method, Davis later wrote,

> I added some other kind of sound I remembered from being back in Arkansas when we were walking home from church and they were playing these...gospels. So that kind of feeling came back to me and I started remembering what that music sounded like and felt like. That feeling is what I was trying to get close to. That feeling had got into my creative blood, my imagination, and I had forgotten it was there.[1]

The album that resulted from this inspiration was called "Kind of Blue," and, almost from the time it was released, it was recognized as a masterpiece. Evans's haunting, impressionistic accompaniment left plenty of space for Davis, Coltrane, and Adderley to invent freely as they never did— or never could—before. Coltrane's impassioned, insistent voice emerges in all its burning-coal intensity. Pianist Wynton Kelly (1931–1971), who had replaced Evans in the band shortly before these sessions, sat in only for one cut, "Freddie Freeloader."

Davis's glamour and renown helped galvanize audiences to this new approach. He and the other "Kind of Blue" musicians, notably Coltrane, Adderley, and Evans, would continue exploring the ramifications of that March 1959 session well beyond their tenures with Davis's group.

The biggest change was yet to come. Two months after the "Kind of Blue" sessions, four musicians met in a Los Angeles recording studio to record jazz music so different that, for a time afterward, some refused to consider it jazz at all.

It was an interesting group. Bassist Charlie Haden (1937–) came from a musical family who played bluegrass and "hillbilly gospel" on the radio. Trumpeter Don Cherry (1936–) sang gospel with his family in a Watts Baptist church on Sundays while helping his father tend bar at a Los Angeles jazz club the rest of the week. Drummer Billy Higgins (1936–) had made a name throughout the L.A. area for his versatility and precision.

The leader—armed with a white plastic alto saxophone soon to become as famous as its owner—was Ornette Coleman (1930–) who was so inspired by the R&B bands playing in his native Fort Worth, Texas, that he joined one when he was fourteen. The robust, hard-riffing sound of those bands made a lasting impression on Coleman even as he took on the more technical challenges of bebop. That he did this while still playing straight-ahead blues music was just one indication of Coleman's nonconformist spirit.

He also wore a beard and long, straightened hair at a time when such a look wasn't the norm. In 1949, while touring Baton Rouge, Louisiana, with a blues band, Coleman was beaten by a gang of roughnecks who didn't like the way he looked nor the sounds he was playing on his tenor sax, which they threw away in the melée.[2]

As a result, Coleman was stranded in New Orleans without a horn. He spent several months living with the family of a trumpeter and found a kindred spirit in a local drummer named Ed Blackwell (1929–1992), who was working out some new possibilities for rhythm within traditional New Orleans march-style percussion. It was the kind of mix of modernism and tradition that Coleman was trying to achieve. After a decade of work with R&B stars like Ray Charles and Earl King, Blackwell became Coleman's regular drummer in 1960.

By the mid-fifties, Coleman was in Los Angeles, looking for music gigs, studying books on harmony and theory, and taking odd jobs like operating an elevator. Eventually, he met other musicians like Haden and Cherry, who were also looking for new ways to break free of jazz conventions. The essence of what they were looking for was summed up by Haden more than twenty years later: "This particular language of improvisation is playing on the tune of the composition rather than on the chord structure." Before meeting Coleman, Haden recalled wanting to play with "the *feeling* of the piece" rather than with the harmonies.[3] As Coleman himself would put it, "Let's play the music, not the background."[4]

Coleman, Haden, Cherry, and Blackwell began working together on their ideas with other sympathetic musicians like Higgins. Some of the pieces that Coleman had been tinkering with since his R&B days were recorded in 1958 on his first album, "Something Else!: The Music of Ornette Coleman." By this time, word was beginning to spread among musicians, critics, and listeners about Coleman's music.

The revolution arrived in earnest with the May 1959 sessions, which were collected and released later that year in an album entitled "The Shape of Jazz to Come." To those accustomed to more conventional jazz, the music on this landmark album can still unsettle with its seemingly chaotic delivery. Once these casual or unwary listeners believe they've latched onto a groove or riff, the quartet shifts gears, melodically, harmonically, emotionally. But, as with "Kind of Blue," the music assumes a logic of its own.

Many listeners at the time were completely put off by this new music, finding it strange, even ugly. But just as many listeners embraced Coleman's music, finding not ugliness so much as new forms of beauty.

Within the jazz community, lines were drawn between pro- and anti-Coleman forces. The new music found its greatest support, ironically, among formalists like John Lewis, leader of the Modern Jazz Quartet, and classical musicians like Leonard Bernstein. Much of the anti-Coleman faction was made up of jazz artists like Roy Eldridge ("I think he's putting everybody on"),[5] Dizzy Gillespie, and Miles Davis, whose much-quoted put-down of Coleman linked the sounds coming out of his saxophone with someone who was "all screwed up inside."[6]

Even Charles Mingus, whose own work helped pave the way for the new music, in later years became skeptical of what would come to be called "free jazz." Yet, Eric Dolphy (1928–1964), one of the musicians playing with Mingus near the start of the 1960s, was sympathetic enough to what Coleman was doing to join the altoist on the 1960 album "Free Jazz." (Dolphy was a virtuoso saxophonist, flutist, and bass clarinetist who came from the same L.A. music scene that nurtured both Coleman and Mingus.)

When "Free Jazz" was released, its cover was decorated with a painting by the abstract expressionist Jackson Pollack. And the music inside has the same seemingly haphazard artistry. People still debate the merits of this music. But there was little doubt that a door had been opened by Ornette Coleman and his followers that couldn't be closed again.

Others who were shaping new sounds at about the same time as Coleman were pulled into public recognition by the free jazz furor. By far, the most exotic of these experimentalists was Herman "Sonny" Blount (1914–1992), a pianist-bandleader who worked with Fletcher Henderson in Chicago's Club De Lisa during the early 1940s. Toward the end of the decade, he started organizing his own bands with players garbed in wild costumes. Some of them played instruments from Africa and the Far East along with the standard horns and saxes.

By the fifties, Blount, who had adopted the name Sun Ra, added electronic instruments to the mix. Much of the music Sun Ra and his "Arkestras" played in these years sounded very much in the hard-bop vein but with themes, moods, and melodies derived from science fiction. The Arkestra's mix of cosmic spectacle and rough-edged music soon won a small, but devoted cult of fans who stayed with the imperious, outrageous leader through several decades of playing both "inside" and "outside" conventional jazz.

Ra left Chicago for New York in 1961 to carry his experiments even further. The "Second City," however, soon harbored a new wave of musical adventurers. In 1965, pianist-composer Muhal Richard Abrams (1930–), who for the previous four years had been running a combination rehearsal band and experimental academy for budding free jazz players, helped establish the Association for the Advancement of Creative Musicians (AACM), a cooperative of progressive-minded musicians seeking artistic and economic freedom.

While the free jazz movement was building momentum, the possibilities for modal jazz continued to be mined by those inspired by "Kind of Blue." With his 1962 album, "Let Freedom Ring," alto saxophonist Jackie McLean declared independence from what he called "overused chord progressions," while pianist Andrew Hill (1937–) merged modal improvisations with the kind of off-center rhythmic designs pioneered by Thelonious Monk.

Bill Evans, leaving Miles Davis's group, pursued his own romantic, impressionistic vision with drummer Paul Motian (1931–) and bassist Scott La Faro (1936–1961), who had also played on Coleman's "Free Jazz" album. Evans was shaken by La Faro's death in a car crash. But he recovered and continued to influence generations of jazz musicians moved (at times, to tears) by his sensitivity and grace.

By the mid-1960s, Davis himself would embark on some more intriguing journeys along the path he had cleared. Accompanying him were saxophonist Wayne Shorter (1933–), pianist Herbie Hancock (1940–), bassist Ron Carter (1937–), and drummer Tony Williams (1945–). In a series of records, beginning with 1965's "E.S.P.," this quintet made impressionistic pictures with sound. Slippery rhythms and knotty, enigmatic melodies would distinguish this unit, thanks, in large part, to Shorter's compositions, whose unpredictability was well suited to Davis's keen sense of drama. This quintet made the kind of music that seduced you and kept you guessing at the same time.

Although Davis's influence remained considerable throughout the 1960s, it was his former sideman, John Coltrane, who dominated the decade in jazz. Many jazz listeners were drawn to Coltrane's passionate pursuit of his artistic grail. Just what that grail was might have been a mystery to him as well as to his fans and his detractors. But the quest itself continues to inspire listeners and musicians who learned to believe in jazz's transfiguring power from listening to Coltrane play.

As a twelve-year-old in North Carolina, Coltrane was given a clarinet to play. By 1944, when his family had moved to Philadelphia, he was also playing alto sax. During a navy stint, he played bebop with an Armed Services jazz band. He switched to a tenor saxophone when, in 1947, he joined blues sax player Eddie "Cleanhead" Vinson's band.

He apprenticed with the bands of Dizzy Gillespie, Johnny Hodges, and Earl Bostic, from the late 1940s through the early 1950s. His renown was limited to the Philadelphia jazz scene until he got a call from Miles Davis in 1955 to join a newly formed quintet. The bristly sound of Coltrane's sax put off many listeners and critics at first, but audiences drawn to the group by Davis's star power began to warm to "Trane's" intensity and passion, especially on ballads.

Still, it wasn't until after the summer of 1957, when Coltrane had cleaned himself of his drug-and-alcohol habits and worked with Thelonious Monk, that a commanding assurance could be heard in his solos. In 1958, jazz critic Ira Gitler coined a phrase that would become the most oft-

John Coltrane

used description of Coltrane's torrential style: "sheets of sound."

Though Coltrane was rid of his more debilitating vices, the insatiable appetite that Miles Davis had seen in his tenor's personality had been transferred to a headlong pursuit of higher spiritual values and musical ideas. Such hunger intensified a furiously inventive style that prompted many musicians and critics to declare Coltrane, by the end of the 1950s, the true artistic heir to Charlie Parker.

Coltrane continued to play with Davis's quintet and on his own albums. His restlessness with Davis was apparent on his last European tour with the trumpeter in March 1960. Coltrane's soloing on a recording of a concert in Sweden that month sounds as if he were half a world away from the rest of the quintet.

One hears in these solos evidence of Coltrane's interest in the music of India with its incantatory melodies. Coltrane pursued this interest later that year on one of his most popular albums, "My Favorite Things." The title track, taken from Rodgers and Hammerstein's musical of the period, "The Sound of Music," was transformed by Coltrane's soprano sax solo into what sounds like an extended meditation on the nature of joy.

It was also on this album that Coltrane began solidifying the quartet that would become the decade's most celebrated jazz unit. Pianist McCoy Tyner (1938–) provided a potent combination of surging lyricism and rhythmic drive. Drummer Elvin Jones (1927–) played with an abandon that both matched and complemented the leader's own. Eventually, this group was rounded out by bassist Jimmy Garrison (1934–1976). With this quartet, Coltrane intensified his search for new sounds. While continuing his experiments with modes and scales, he also exchanged ideas with Ornette Coleman and members of his groundbreaking band. Even more than Coleman, Coltrane was accused of playing his horn with calculated harshness. One prominent jazz critic even accused Coltrane's early 1960s music of being "ugly on purpose."

There were also those who heard in Coltrane's tempestuous sound a sustained musical response to centuries of racial injustice. Coltrane's emergence as a major jazz figure coincided with the civil rights movement and the concurrent surge of self-pride within the African-American community. Many made a direct connection between the harsh urgency in Coltrane's music and the pent-up rage of black Americans. These connections emerged tellingly on "Alabama," a mournful ballad performed by Coltrane's quartet at Birdland in November 1963, inspired by the bombing, two months before, of a Birmingham, Alabama, Baptist church in which four black children were killed.

Rarely was Coltrane as directly political in his music. Asked once whether there was an analogy between his music and the black nationalist rhetoric of Malcolm X, Coltrane replied, "Well, I think that music being an expression of the human heart, or of the human being itself, does express just what is happening. I just feel it expresses the whole thing—the whole of human experience at the particular time it is being expressed."[7]

Indeed the anger that many heard in Coltrane's playing was almost completely at odds with his personality. Friends remember him as a gentle, soft-spoken man with an almost childlike affection for beauty in art and music. The deep spirituality he acquired during his 1957 summer of renewal and recovery was given its boldest rendering in the 1964 album "A Love Supreme," which also was the culmination of everything Coltrane had done—or would ever do—with modal improvisation.

The following year, Coltrane became a full-fledged member of the free-jazz revolution with the album "Ascension." As with Coleman's "Free Jazz," the musicians assembled for this session—among them, trumpeter Freddie Hubbard (1938–) and saxophonists Archie Shepp (1937–)

and Pharaoh Sanders (1940–) seem to be playing in random bursts of spontaneity, creating a fiery cauldron of chaotic noise.

The musicians play off a short series of notes Coltrane sends out at the very beginning. The phrases and solos resulting from Coltrane's brief riff sometimes seem to run into each other. At other times, they seem to be running away from anything resembling a coherent pattern. Yet, however dense or rambling the piece may seem, it stays close to Coltrane's opening theme, like any traditional jazz piece.

Coltrane lost some of his following when he took this new direction. Yet he was such a big star that the fact that he had moved toward free jazz increased the attention it received. Shepp and Sanders, for instance, emerged from "Ascension"'s fiery wake with greater renown. A playwright, poet, and activist, Shepp enhanced the social and political context of the free jazz movement with pieces like "Poem for Malcolm," a tribute to Malcolm X, the black nationalist slain in 1965. Sanders's keening, wailing style enhanced Coltrane's own ballistic inventions when the latter formed his last musical group.

To the end of his life, John Coltrane continued to explore the edges of free jazz while looking for unifying elements to contain, without smothering, its expression. His last album, a series of duets with drummer Rashied Ali called "Interstellar Space," was recorded in February 1967 and seemed close to achieving this difficult synthesis. But before he could take these discoveries to the next level, Coltrane died in August of liver cancer. He was forty years old.

After Armstrong, Ellington, Parker, and Davis, John Coltrane was one of the dominant forces influencing jazz's first century. It is unlikely that the music will have another such hero before the century ends. What seems more likely is that Coltrane's music, as it endures beyond the turbulent era in which it was created, will someday be embraced as an expression not of rage or anxiety, but of joy, exaltation, and wonder.

eleven

ROCK AND RETRENCHMENT

THE SUMMER that John Coltrane died was a season of race riots in Newark and Detroit. At the same time, Americans were fighting and dying in the Vietnam War, while many in the country were demonstrating against the nation's involvement in that war. The era's greatest activist, the Reverend Martin Luther King, Jr., urged America's leaders to direct the nation's energies away from waging war abroad to fighting poverty and injustice at home. Throughout the country, young people were challenging status quo values in many ways, whether by wearing their hair longer or living in communes.

In this time of social, political, and cultural upheaval, jazz struggled to maintain a following. In many cities, jazz musicians took their music to poor neighborhoods to reach audiences who could not afford to attend live concerts or nightclubs. The most celebrated of these programs was New York's Jazzmobile, founded in 1965 by a group of jazz musicians led by Billy Taylor (1921–), a pianist, composer, and bandleader, who is also one of jazz's best-known educators. Jazzmobile took summer jazz concerts to Harlem, the Bronx, Brooklyn, and other New York neighborhoods on a mobile stage. The program also offered classes in music, dance, drama, and art to young people.

But though Jazzmobile and programs like it became established institutions in their communities, they couldn't prevent jazz from being consigned to the margins of popular culture. Rock and roll had seized the imagination of millions of young people who thirty or forty years earlier would have been drawn to jazz and swing. As far as these listeners were concerned, the energy in black music belonged in the 1960s to soul singers like Aretha Franklin, James Brown, and Otis Redding—as well as that corporate giant of black pop, Motown.

Even Miles Davis was finding himself drawn less to his own repertoire of standards and more to the music of Brown, Sly and the Family Stone, and Jimi Hendrix (1943–1970). Their colorful, audacious extensions of blues guitar traditions, advanced under rock's gaudy banner, were as influential as the innovations of Coleman and Coltrane.

Beginning with 1968's "Miles in the Sky," Davis's albums were driven by electrically amplified grooves. The following year, "In a Silent Way" was released, bearing the same kind of mystery and portent that accompanied "Kind of Blue" a decade before. Three of the members of Davis's quintet, Wayne Shorter, Herbie Hancock, and Tony Williams, had decided to help Davis forge what would, before long, be called "fusion" music for its attempts to merge rock with jazz.

Also on this album were two electric keyboard players joining Hancock. Joe Zawinul (1932–) was an Austrian émigré who, while with Cannonball Adderley's mid-1960s combo, wrote the soul-jazz anthem "Mercy, Mercy, Mercy." Chick Corea (1941–) apprenticed with Latin bands in the sixties. Both bassist Dave Holland (1946–) and guitarist

John McLaughlin (1942–) built reputations in their native England before getting the call from Davis.

"In a Silent Way" set the stage for "Bitches Brew," released the following year, which was Davis's most commercially successful album. As with "Kind of Blue," Davis had only sketched-out versions of what he wanted his musicians to play during the "Brew" recording sessions. "It was just like one of them old-time jam sessions we used to have up at Minton's," Davis later recalled. "Everybody was excited when we left there each day."[1]

Still, it was clear from "Bitches Brew"'s success that, for Davis, Minton's and everything that went with it was long gone. Davis now performed only at rock clubs, coliseums, and other pop music venues. Many jazz loyalists felt deserted, even betrayed, by Davis. They saw his move to fusion as a cynical bid for younger record buyers.

Davis made no attempt to hide his yearning for the ears of young people, especially young African Americans. His 1972 album, "On the Corner," was charged with the hard-core funk of James Brown and Sly Stone. It also exploited a creative tension of space and sound characteristic of Davis's best music. Davis even began to acknowledge that Ornette Coleman may have been right "about things being played three or four ways independently of each other."[2]

Meanwhile, many of the musicians who played with Davis on "In a Silent Way" became stars, bringing amplified instruments and electronic synthesizers to the jazz marketplace. Herbie Hancock's early forays into amplified funk-jazz culminated with the 1973 best-seller "Headhunters." Zawinul and Shorter became the twin poles governing one fusion ensemble, Weather Report. With his supercharged Mahavishnu orchestra, John McLaughlin had become almost as big an influence on electric guitar as Jimi Hendrix.

Much of the lush romanticism and dramatic tension of amplified jazz fusion could be found in the acoustic piano jazz of the early to mid-1970s. Keith Jarrett (1943–), who had been a sideman with Art Blakey, Miles Davis, and tenor saxophonist Charles Lloyd, went from cult status to international fame through solo piano recitals weaving elements of jazz, soul, rock, and classical music into colorful, impressionistic tapestries. Corea alternated work with his Return to Power fusion band with acoustic piano performances that displayed his flair for bright melody and beguiling whimsy.

That Scott Joplin's ragtime piano music enjoyed a modest revival in the early 1970s only enhanced the pace-setting prominence of pianists like Hancock, Jarrett, and Corea. McCoy Tyner, who had helped John Coltrane make jazz history a decade before, was a beneficiary of this trend with a series of successful albums that made him a top draw in clubs, concert halls, and colleges. Working well beyond fusion's boundaries, Tyner played the piano with a fiery, near-incantatory power reminiscent of his late employer. Yet, in solo, small ensemble, or big-band settings, Tyner's style was celebrated for its own density and passion.

The most unexpected piano hero of this period was Cecil Taylor. Carried along by the same avant-garde wave that bore Coleman, Coltrane, and others to prominence in the 1960s, Taylor began the 1970s tucked away in a university, teaching, writing, and conducting a student big band. Beginning in 1973, he recorded a series of solo albums, notably "Indent," "Silent Tongues," and "Spring of Two Blue Js," that provided compelling showcases for Taylor's tumultuous imagination. In its reach for new ideas, Taylor's music became a genre unto itself.

Like Taylor, Ornette Coleman, avatar of the 1960s' "free jazz" movement, remained true through the 1970s to his questing impulses. He began the decade with a twenty-one-movement piece for alto saxophone and symphony orchestra, "Skies of America," which was recorded in 1972. The liner notes of the album provide Coleman's first

Cecil Taylor

mention of his "Harmolodic Theory, which uses melody, harmony, and the instrumentation of the movement of forms."

No one, not even Coleman, has come up with a simple definition of "harmolodics," which *seems* to define the combination of broad resources and an open mind that a musician needs to play "free" in a group setting. "Skies of America" was the first experiment in such collective free thinking. By the late seventies, Coleman had formed an electronic band, Prime Time, which has served since then as a major outlet for his always provocative ideas.

The popularity of fusion, and the concurrent interest in acoustic piano music in the early 1970s, seemed to send mixed signals about the state of jazz music. In fact, jazz's energies after John Coltrane's death seemed scattered in several directions, groping for an elusive foundation. As the decade went on, however, it became clear that the only constant in jazz was *eclecticism*, meaning that musicians were finding their styles in many different sources—like rock, or classical, or blues music.

This flexibility was not new to the music. From the turn of the century, jazz grew from a convergence of musical forms, blues and ragtime making up the first such "fusion." As it evolved, jazz was open to many musical idioms here and throughout the world. Rhythms from Africa and the Caribbean, melodies and instrumentation from India and, especially during the mid-sixties, Brazilian samba, had become woven into the language of jazz. From the French Gypsy guitarist Django Reinhardt (1910–1953) to the Japanese pianist-bandleader Toshiko Akiyoshi (1929–), from the Argentinean tenor saxophonist Gato Barbieri (1933–), to the South African pianist-composer Abdullah Ibrahim (1934–), musicians on many continents have made strong and enduring contributions to the development of this African-American art form.

What made the 1970s different from previous jazz

eras—and, in some ways, set the tone for the decades to come—was that little forward movement of the music resulted from the varied experiments with rock and electronics. The eclecticism of the 1970s heralded an age of retrenchment and reexamination in jazz.

Not even the so-called "cutting-edge" of the music was immune to eclectic impulses. But what distinguished the music of the seventies avant-garde from fusion's romantic mix-masters was its willingness to reach deep into jazz's past. Marching-band arrangements, ragtime, blues, even yodels and tribal chants, inspired much of the 1970s' experimental music.

These experiments were conducted in lofts, abandoned factories, and other performing spaces more hospitable to exploration than nightclubs and concert halls. This "loft scene" included musicians who had either played with or been inspired by Chicago's Association for the Advancement of Creative Music. Muhal Richard Abrams, one of AACM's founders, built many of his experiments in jazz structure with a strong foundation in traditional forms like stride, rag, blues, and bop.

Much like Monk, Anthony Braxton (1945–), another AACM alumnus, challenged formal jazz elements by imposing a kind of counter-form allowing for greater range of improvisation. The titles of Braxton's cerebral compositions tended to look like mathematical formulas and geometric diagrams, and the music ranged from tightly packed phrases to frenzied bursts of pure inspiration.

The wildest product of the AACM was the Art Ensemble of Chicago, which began in 1969 as a drumless unit consisting of trumpeter Lester Bowie (1941–), saxophonists Joseph Jarman (1937–) and Roscoe Mitchell (1940–), and bassist Malachi Favors (1937–). Later, percussionist Famoudou Don Moye (1946–) was added.

In all of jazz history, it's unlikely that any musical group

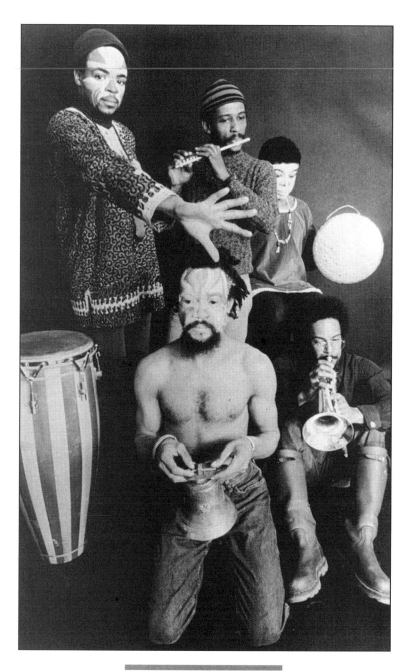

The Chicago Art Ensemble

has matched the Art Ensemble in stage presence. Bowie, for instance, wore a laboratory coat while Moye, Jarman, and Favors often wore African garb and painted face designs. The music they played was just as flamboyant and unorthodox. Bells, whistles, spoken poetry, and drums of all sizes were part of the show. The Art Ensemble became internationally famous for an abstract, improvised black music that never strayed far from the basics of blues and the beat—or from an impious sense of fun.

Another midwestern musicians' collective, the Black Artists Group, was founded in St. Louis in 1968 with the same goals as AACM's. Many creative musicians emerged from that group, but three in particular would go on to form one of the most distinctive ensembles of the late 1970s: baritone saxophonist Hamiet Bluiett (1938–), alto saxophonist Julius Hemphill (1940–), soprano and tenor saxophonist Oliver Lake (1944–).

Bluiett, Hemphill, and Lake joined tenor saxophonist David Murray (1955–) in 1977 to form the World Saxophone Quartet (WSQ). This unusual ensemble, which performed and recorded with no rhythm section, began by experimenting with different harmonic voicings and sound mixtures. In the 1980s, the WSQ broadened its repertoire to include classics by Duke Ellington and Billy Strayhorn, and rhythm-and-blues standards like Otis Redding's "Dock of the Bay" and Marvin Gaye's "Let's Get It On."

All four WSQ members achieved individual success as composers and performers. Of the four, Murray emerged in the eighties as, perhaps, jazz's most protean player of the era—and certainly its most prolific recording artist. In addition to his work with the WSQ, Murray has performed as leader of several small ensembles and big bands. To date, more than 150 albums have been released under Murray's name.

It has often been written of Murray that you can hear the whole history of tenor saxophone in his playing. And at his most inspired, Murray evokes the force of Coleman

Hawkins, the warmth of Ben Webster, the cleverness of Sonny Rollins, and the wailing abandon of Albert Ayler.

Such a mixture has made Murray's body of work one of the most unpredictable in today's jazz. In one tune, he can explore the outer realms of "free" playing. In another, he can handle down-home swing with the best R&B "honkers." (Indeed, Murray, as a teenager in Berkeley, California, played with a soul-funk combo called "The Notations of Soul.") Murray also plays bass clarinet and is considered the most innovative force on that instrument since Eric Dolphy.

Amid the experimentation and eclecticism of the mid-seventies, many young musicians remained drawn to traditional jazz forms like hard bop and swing. Trumpeter Jon Faddis (1953–), who idolized Dizzy Gillespie, apprenticed himself to his hero and played with the same high-altitude virtuosity. Alto saxophonist Bobby Watson (1954–), meanwhile, sought out Art Blakey in the mid-1970s and eventually became part of the legendary Messengers band in 1977.

Watson had been with Blakey for three years when trumpeter Wynton Marsalis (1961–), a nineteen-year-old classically trained prodigy from New Orleans, joined the Messengers. A Juilliard School of Music student, Marsalis grew up in a musical household. His father, Ellis, was a celebrated jazz pianist and teacher who instilled in his three sons respect for the hard-bop tradition. Branford Marsalis (1960–), Ellis's oldest son, played tenor saxophone with the same confidence and command of bop as Wynton.

But it was the second son whose breakout performances with the Blakey band seemed to revitalize hard bop's possibilities for connecting with a large audience. With the release of Blakey's 1981 "Album of the Year," word spread through the jazz world of the young horn player with the "chops" and the attitude to assert the legitimacy of traditional jazz. His performances at jazz festivals held throughout the country during the summer of 1982 made

Wynton Marsalis the hottest young trumpet player in decades. Within two years, he won Grammys for both jazz and classical recordings.

Traditionalists embraced Marsalis as a savior, describing his and his colleagues' work as a "neoclassical" movement. Others less charitably called it "neoconservative," a label borrowed from politics referring, loosely, to those who advocated liberal or revolutionary social changes in the 1960s, only to renounce such values in the 1980s.

Whatever his politics, Wynton Marsalis assumed, with vigor and pugnacity, the role of defending bop and other idioms abandoned by a generation of jazz musicians. In the process, he publicly criticized musicians who had allied themselves with fusion or free jazz. Miles Davis, whose influence many had heard in Marsalis's early playing, came in for an especially heavy attack from Marsalis.

Davis, who had retired in 1975 because of health problems, made a comeback in the same year as Marsalis's breakthrough. He seemed weakened by his bouts with physical ailments, but his tone sounded, if anything, more robust. As cocksure and swaggering onstage as ever, Davis picked up where he'd left off, backed by musicians setting down thick cushions of amplified funky rhythms. Ironically, Marsalis was drawing accolades for playing the kind of music Davis abandoned nearly fifteen years before.

Davis had no desire to head back to that music. Indeed, with his return to active performing, Davis seemed more determined than ever to connect with mainstream audiences. In 1985, he recorded "You're under Arrest," an album of contemporary standards, including Michael Jackson's "Human Nature." He was becoming more intrigued with hip-hop and rap and, toward the end of his life, was attempting to merge such forms with jazz.

Through all of Davis's restless search for new "fusions," one thing remained constant: the plaintive voice pouring from the bell of his horn. Davis remained, to the end, a

Wynton Marsalis

blues-singing instrumentalist who, like Billie Holiday, Louis Armstrong, or Lester Young, could create a world of feeling with the simplest sound.

Since Davis's death, in 1991, of a stroke, much of the effort to bring jazz and hip-hop together has come from the latter end of the mix. Hip-hop artists like Guru, A Tribe Called Quest, Digable Planets, and US3 have been throwing prerecorded "samples" of jazz music into their recordings. It's too soon to tell what will result from such experiments. Yet no one should dismiss any honest effort to align jazz music with popular dancing. Who can say what creative possibilities will be pried open by the hip-hop beat?

Wynton Marsalis had nothing against the soul-funk music of his teenage years. The music press made much of brother Branford's decision, in 1985, to leave Wynton's group to join rock star Sting's first band, but it marked no serious rift between the brothers, whose commercial success inspired scores of younger players to apply their talents to the long-abandoned hard-bop idiom. (Indeed, Branford Marsalis had one of his biggest commercial successes with "Trio Jeepy," a 1988 album of jazz standards.) Still, with his popularity and his high-profile status as artistic director of the Jazz at Lincoln Center program, Wynton Marsalis was the most conspicuous symbol of jazz's ongoing era of conservatism and retrenchment.

Yet within the boundaries he defined for himself as a musician, Marsalis was as artistically restless as any avant-garde adventurer. By the mid-eighties, he was edging away from the stylish and slippery hard-bop music that made him famous. He recorded a series of albums in 1988 that dealt with the blues and the music of his native New Orleans. (One album was released later that year under the title "The Majesty of the Blues." Three others were released in 1991 under the rubric "Soul Gestures in Southern Blue.") Marsalis's interest in Ellington's music has also inspired him to attempt orchestral works with the maestro's thematic ambition. One such work, "CITI Movement," was originally written in 1992 for the choreographer Garth Fagan. More recent compositions include, "In This House/On This Morning" (1992), a work inspired by black church rituals, "Jazz: Six Syncopated Movements" (1993), a ballet celebrating American music, and "Blood on the Fields" (1994), a long piece about African-American slavery.

After Marsalis left the Blakey band, Terence Blanchard (1962–) took the trumpeter's chair. Like Marsalis, Blanchard hailed from New Orleans and he, too, would achieve renown for his technical facility. Later, Blanchard became just as famous for writing film scores, one of which was the critically acclaimed accompaniment to Spike Lee's 1991 epic, *Malcolm X*. From this score, Blanchard fashioned "The Malcolm X Suite," a series of themes and riffs from the film converted for small combo.

Another path was taken by Marcus Roberts (1963–) who was a pianist in Wynton Marsalis's mid-1980s ensemble. Roberts has moved almost exclusively toward mastering the repertoire of classic jazz. Many of his albums thus far have been solo piano recitals of works by Jelly Roll Morton, James P. Johnson, and Thelonious Monk. His own work for piano and big band resonates with references to Ellington and Monk.

Roberts's ties with past masters have fueled the complaints of those seeking more adventurous destinies for jazz. Yet it is hard not to feel heartened by young black musicians tending to the best of what their predecessors had created with such attentive and informed care.

Marsalis's Jazz at Lincoln Center program is at the forefront of the jazz repertory movement. This trend originated in many college, university, and high school jazz curriculums that have developed in the last couple of decades. In the mid-1980s, the New York–based American Jazz Orchestra mounted concerts featuring the music of such composers and arrangers as Benny Carter and Duke Ellington.

Since the 1990s began, major cultural organizations like the Smithsonian Institution, Lincoln Center, Carnegie Hall, and the John F. Kennedy Center for the Performing Arts have started programs to preserve jazz's glorious past and to help perpetuate its future. Repertory orchestras at these and other organizations have presented the music of the established masters and of those who have been short-changed or neglected.

The reputations of both Duke Ellington and Charles Mingus have benefited from this restorative spirit. Some of Ellington's more obscure work has been brought to light by repertory bands like the Lincoln Center Jazz Orchestra, startling audiences with its radiance, subtlety, and emotional variety.

The Charles Mingus revival began in 1989, ten years after his death, with a highly acclaimed performance of "Epitaph," an orchestral work whose failure, when first presented in 1962, was a shattering episode in the bassist-composer's life. The revival has continued through the Mingus Big Band, which plays weekly at a New York nightclub to enthusiastic audiences. Many younger listeners new to jazz music have said they find, in Mingus's passionate, volatile music, some of rock and roll's grand intensity. Other composers and arrangers will also be rediscovered over the next several decades, as jazz takes stock of its past.

Whatever acclaim and excitement such revivalism generates, it also arouses concern over whether jazz, as an art form, has stopped growing. This worry has been increased by the deaths in recent years of a number of major artists: Miles Davis, Dizzy Gillespie, Art Blakey, Stan Getz, Sun Ra, Sarah Vaughan, Ed Blackwell, and Billy Eckstine. Their contributions to the music's development were enormous and lasting. But who, many wondered, will carry on after their achievements?

There are many answers to be drawn from several generations of musicians. Sonny Rollins and J. J. Johnson, for instance, continue to record and perform with youthful agility. Cecil Taylor still summons ferocious storms from a piano keyboard. Ornette Coleman still searches for new ways to relate to harmony.

The career of singer Betty Carter (1929–) is the most singular in contemporary jazz. She sang with the Lionel Hampton band in the late 1940s and early 1950s. She went on to record several albums, including a memorable 1958 duet with Ray Charles. Along with a buttery smooth intonation, Carter brought to jazz singing the same level of invention found in Monk and Parker. During the 1970s, Carter formed her own label, Bet-Car, which allowed her to pursue her artistic goals without interference from a major record company. Twelve albums were recorded under the Bet-Car label. It faded, wrote critic-historian Will Friedwald, "because as good a businesswoman as Carter is, she's not good enough to run an independent jazz label."[3] In the late 1980s, she recorded a series of albums with Verve records, establishing her preeminence among living jazz singers.

What's more, Carter has served as mentor to more important musicians than any singer since Billy Eckstine— and, perhaps, any bandleader since Art Blakey. Among the accompanists who have been nurtured to stardom by Carter's guidance are pianists John Hicks, Benny Green, Stephen Scott, Cyrus Chestnut, and Jacky Terrasson, and the drummers Kenny Washington and Gregory Hutchinson.

In recent years, many older musicians whose work was relatively unnoticed in the shadows of the giants have become major figures. Among these late bloomers is tenor saxophonist Joe Henderson (1937–), whose successful tribute albums to Billy Strayhorn and Miles Davis in the early 1990s brought wide appreciation for his conceptual abilities.

Henry Threadgill (1944–) expanded the possibilities of jazz orchestration with his Very Very Circus, an ensemble using two amplified guitars, two tubas, and a French horn along with Threadgill's alto sax and various sets of drums.

Betty Carter

This unusual combination creates music vibrant enough to make the listener feel like marching or dancing.

Threadgill is prominent among those clearing a separate path from the traditionalism of Marsalis and his followers. There are other bold and clever eclecticists who are so much at home in varied musical genres that they see no major difference in the possibilities they offer. These musicians include the clarinetist Don Byron, who first drew attention playing in bands specializing in Jewish *klezmer* music. He has also recorded with rock bands and brought innovative energy to jazz clarinet.

Saxophonist Steve Coleman (1955–), pianist Geri Allen (1957–), and singer Cassandra Wilson (1956–) share Byron's ease with different musical idioms. All three were part of Brooklyn's "M-Base" musical collective that, during the 1980s, tried to establish a link between jazz and the rhythms of funk masters like James Brown and George Clinton. They have found the music of Motown as usable as that of Coltrane, Ellington, and Monk, and have proved themselves able to do solid work using all aspects of the black musical tradition. Such boundary-breaching attitudes could evolve into one of the many shapes jazz assumes in its second century.

Despite all this activity, there are those who believe that jazz is nothing more than a form of popular music that stopped being *really* popular about forty years ago.

But, the music has endured and even thrived. Though its energies now seem scattered, jazz, by whatever name or means, will continue to evolve—like all other living things.

As Thelonious Monk once said when asked where jazz was "going": "You can't make anything go anywhere. It just happens."

twelve

CODA

FUN IS A WORD that occasionally appears in this book. I'm not sure it's emphasized enough. Yes, jazz can inspire, enrich, comfort, and ennoble the human spirit. It is also is a form of *play*. Why does a singer take the lyric of a song and makes it sound different? What makes trumpeters or saxophonists decide that they don't have to keep to the beat of a tune in the same way? Because they *can*.

Jazz offers any musician the opportunity to invent, even reinvent, melody, harmony, and rhythm to fit his or her personality. It's this sense of freedom and possibility that excites people to this day about Louis Armstrong's first recordings with King Oliver, or Lester Young's quick-witted solos with Count Basie's band. What comes through on these and other recorded performances is a bold assertion of self within a group setting. When Armstrong lets loose a shining stream of high notes in the middle of a song, it's not much different from a basketball star like Michael Jordan or Charles Barkley gliding or carving his way through an opposing team's defense to make a spectacularly effective move to the basket.

Play. That you can be yourself while remaining connected with your community is an ideal jazz music shares with democracy itself. When America's Founders built a republic dedicated to offering its citizens "life, liberty and the pursuit of happiness," none of them could imagine they were describing the very things an African-American musical form offers both its artists and listeners—especially that "pursuit of happiness" part. A sense of play can be found even in the performances of an artist like Billie Holiday, for whom life wasn't always "fun."

As a listener, you are as much a "player" as the singers or musicians. You bring your own feelings to a performer's work the way a performer puts everything he or she has into a song. This is true of all music, but what makes jazz especially exciting is that your own reactions can be as unpredictable as the music. It isn't necessary to understand the technical aspects of what a musician is doing. Often, you find your own meaning to a piece of music.

Perhaps the meaning will find *you.* An example: Once I was riding a rented bicycle across an island. It was hot. The bike was old. I had reached the middle of the island and was feeling tired and thirsty. At the time, I had been listening to Cecil Taylor's solo piano record "Silent Tongues," and I wasn't yet sure what I thought of it. Somehow, an especially intense fragment from that performance filtered into my memory as I was riding the bike up a steep hill. Whatever mix of emotion I was feeling at that moment was matched by what I remembered hearing on that album. Both the music and my ride became vivid to me.

This is the kind of offhand magic that can happen to you when you're listening to or creating jazz music. You find yourself playing with all kinds of ideas and responses whether you prefer New Orleans music, swing, bop, or free jazz.

Keep your ears open. Sample as much of the music as you can. But, more than anything, have fun. And be ready, always, to *play.*

SOURCE NOTES

INTRODUCTION
1. Frank Tirro, *Jazz: A History,* second edition (New York: W. W. Norton & Co., 1993), 97.
2. Langston Hughes, *Jazz,* updated by Sanford Brown (New York: Franklin Watts, 1982), 33–34. Excerpted in *Reading Jazz,* ed. David Meltzer. (San Francisco: Mercury House, 1993), 41–42.
3. Tirro, *Jazz,* 87.

ONE
1. Ortiz M. Walton, *Music: Black, White and Blue* (New York: William Morrow and Co., 1972), 4.
2. Paul Oliver, *Savannah Syncopaters: African Retentions in the Blues* (New York: Stein and Day, 1970), 20.
3. Albert Murray, *Stomping the Blues* (New York: Da Capo Press, 1976), 45.
4. Leonard Feather, *Encyclopedia of Jazz* (New York: Da Capo Press, 1960), 423.
5. Marshall W. Stearns, *The Story of Jazz* (New York: Oxford University Press, 1956, 1958), 160.

TWO

1. Tom Davin, "Conversation with James P. Johnson," *Jazz Panorama*: *From the Pages of Jazz Review* in Martin Williams, ed. (New York: Collier Books, 1964), 45–61.

THREE

1. Marshall W. Stearns, *The Story of Jazz* (New York: Oxford University Press, 1956), 55–56.
2. Nat Shapiro and Nat Hentoff, *Hear Me Talkin' to Ya* (New York: Dover Publications, 1955), 15–16.
3. Alan Lomax, *Mister Jelly Roll* (Berkeley: University of California Press, 1950), 18.
4. Stearns, *Story of Jazz*, 51–54.
5. Lomax, *Mister Jelly Roll*, 60.
6. Louis Armstrong, *Satchmo: My Life in New Orleans* (New York: Da Capo Press, 1954), 23.
7. Lomax, *Mister Jelly Roll*, 64.
8. Ibid., 63.
9. Armstrong, *Satchmo*, 53.
10. Quoted in *The Penguin Guide to Jazz on CD, LP and Cassette* (London: Penguin Books, ed. Richard Cook and Brian Morton, 1992), 86–87.
11. Armstrong, *Satchmo*, 24.

FOUR

1. Louis Armstrong, *Satchmo: My Life in New Orleans* (New York: Da Capo Press, 1954), 150.
2. Gary Giddins, *Satchmo* (New York: Dolphin/Doubleday, 1988), 71.
3. Martin Williams, *The Jazz Tradition* (New York: Oxford University Press, 1970, 1983), 54.

FIVE

1. Rex Stewart, *Jazz Masters of the 30s* (New York: Da Capo Press, 1972), 21–22.
2. Ibid, 22.
3. Richard Cook and Brian Morton, *The Penguin Guide*

to Jazz on CD, LP and Cassette (London: Penguin, 1994), 900.
4. John Edward Hasse, *The World of Duke Ellington* (New York: Simon and Schuster, 1993), 88.
5. Stewart, *Jazz Masters*, 11.
6. Nat Shapiro and Nat Hentoff, *Hear Me Talkin' to Ya* (New York: Holt Rinehart and Winston, 1955), 222.

SIX
1. John Edward Hasse, *Beyond Category: The Life and Genius of Duke Ellington* (New York: Simon and Schuster,1993), 22.
2. Liner notes from "The Smithsonian Collection of Classic Jazz," 1973 edition (Washington, D.C.: Smithsonian Institution), 37.
3. Edward Kennedy "Duke" Ellington, *Music Is My Mistress* (New York: Doubleday, 1973), 156.
4. Hasse, *Beyond Category*, 373.

SEVEN
1. Nat Shapiro and Nat Hentoff, *Hear Me Talking to Ya* (New York: Holt Rinehart and Winston, 1955), 289.
2. Ibid., 284.
3. David McCullough, *Truman* (New York: Simon and Schuster, 1992), 198.
4. Ross Russell, *Jazz Style in Kansas City* (Berkeley: University of California Press, 1971), 136–137.
5. John McDonough, "The Court Martial of Lester Young," *Down Beat*, January 1981, quoted in Lewis Porter, *Lester Young* (Boston: Twayne Publishers, 1985), 24.
6. Porter, *Lester Young*, 25.

EIGHT
1. Gary Giddins, *Celebrating Bird* (New York: Beech Tree Books, 1987), 56.
2. Ibid., 58.
3. Ira Gitler, *Jazz Masters of the Forties* (New York: Collier Books, 1966), 64.

4. Ibid., 70.

5. Leonard Feather, *The Book of Jazz,* rev. ed. (New York: Dell, 1976), 110.

6. Nat Shapiro and Nat Hentoff, *Hear Me Talkin' to Ya* (New York: Holt, Rinehart and Winston, 1955), 374.

7. Ibid., 405.

NINE

1. Arnold Shaw, *Honkers and Shouters: The Golden Years of Rhythm and Blues* (New York: Macmillan, 1978), xvii, 163.

2. Nat Hentoff, *The Jazz Life* (New York: Da Capo Press, 1961), 196.

3. Miles Davis with Quincy Troupe, *Miles: The Autobiography* (New York: Simon and Schuster, 1989), 187.

4. Nat Hentoff, "An Afternoon with Miles Davis," from *Jazz Panorama,* Martin Williams (New York: Collier, 1964), 167.

5. Davis and Troupe, *Miles,* 226.

TEN

1. Miles Davis, with Quincy Troupe, *Miles: The Autobiography* (New York: Simon and Schuster, 1989), 234.

2. A. B. Spellman, *Four Lives in the Bebop Business* (New York: Limelight Editions, 1966, 1985), 100.

3. Quoted by Robert Palmer in booklet accompanying "Beauty Is a Rare Thing: The Complete Atlantic Recordings of Ornette Coleman," released 1993 by Rhino\ Atlantic, 20–22.

4. Martin Williams, *The Jazz Tradition,* 2nd. rev. ed (New York: Oxford University Press, 1993), 235.

5. Palmer, "Beauty Is," 12.

6. Ibid., 19.

7. Frank Kofsky, *Black Nationalism and the Revolution in Music* (New York: Pathfinder Press, 1970), 225.

ELEVEN

1. Miles Davis, with Quincy Troupe, *Miles: The Autobiography* (New York: Simon and Schuster, 1989), 300.
2. Ibid., 322.
3. Will Friedwald, *Jazz Singing* (New York: Macmillan, 1990, 1992), 406.

GLOSSARY

ANTIPHONY Music in which sounds, melodies, phrases "call" and "respond" to each other.

ARPEGGIO The rapid playing of the tones of a chord.

ARRANGER The person who selects the voices and instruments to be used in a musical composition.

AVANT-GARDE A group of artists in any field who seek new techniques and ideas (literally, the advance guard).

BALLAD A simple song.

BEAT, TEMPO Rhythm and timing in music.

BEBOP, BOP Jazz music characterized by virtuoso playing, complex rhythms, and harmonies.

BLUE NOTES Slurred notes somewhere between flat and natural notes.

BOOGIE-WOOGIE A kind of blues played mostly on piano, with a steady rolling beat and a strong deep bass added.

BREAK A brief passage between musical phrases—often improvised in written jazz.

CALL-AND-RESPONSE See antiphony.

CHORD A combination of notes that blend together to make a single sound.

CHORD CHANGES A combination of chords that make up a song's melody. Musicians sometimes improvise new melodies from these changes.

COMBO A small band.

COOL JAZZ A jazz style perceived as subdued, understated, or restrained in expression.

CRESCENDO Sound increasing gradually in volume or intensity.

CUTTING CONTEST, CARVING CONTEST Contests between musicians who got together and tried to outplay each other. One musician would "cut" in and play solo after another musician's solo.

ENSEMBLE A musical band; a trio, quartet, quintent, or a full orchestra.

FUNK, FUNKY Thick, heavily-atmospheric quality; often used to describe African-American blues and jazz that is especially rhythmic or zesty.

FUSION Term used for efforts to merge or "fuse" rock and jazz forms.

GLISSANDO A rapid sliding up and down the musical scale. Louis Armstrong's solos were famous for glissandos.

GOSPEL MUSIC Emotionally stirring religious music linked to the African-American church.

HARMONY A pleasing arrangement of simultaneous sounds.

HARD BOP Bop music with especially thick harmonies, a heavy beat, and themes reminiscent of gospel or rhythm-and-blues.

IDIOM A way of expressing oneself in language, music, or art.

IMPROVISATION Music composed as it is played; also, new variations on old themes.

JAM, JAMMING To get together with other musicians to play (mostly improvise) music.

KEY The tonality of a scale.

MELODY A musical phrase or song; a tune.

MODES Musical scales with special tones or characteristics.

MODAL IMPROVISATION A type of improvising that is done directly from the notes of a musical scale rather than from chord changes.

MUSICAL SCALE A graduated series of musical tones going up or down.

OBLIGATO Musical accompaniment that is vital to a piece. Often, an instrumental solo in the midst of a jazz vocal.

PERCUSSION The beat that drives a musical piece or ensemble. Drums provide percussion; so can a guitar, bass, tuba, or piano.

PHRASE A short musical thought.

POLYPHONY A combination of two or more melodies.

RAP Rhymes spoken to a syncopated beat.

RAGTIME Music driven by rhythms with syncopated melodies and regularly accented beats.

RHYTHM AND BLUES, R&B Blues music characterized by a heavy beat and amplified melodies and riffs.

RIFF A single rhythmic phrase repeated over and over.

SPIRITUAL A religious song developed among southern blacks.

STOP-TIME A "break" in which a soloist sings or plays over a simple rhythmic pattern set down by a pianist or ensemble.

STRIDE PIANO Style of solo jazz piano in which the rhythm seems to be "walking" or "striding."

SYNCOPATION A shifting of accents and stresses from normally strong beats to the weak beats. It often means playing one rhythm against another in such a way that listeners want to move, nod heads, clap hands, or dance. SWING is a form of syncopation; so are ROCK-AND-ROLL and HIP-HOP.

VIRTUOSO A musician who is a master of his or her instrument.

RECOMMENDED BOOKS

Albertson, Chris. *Bessie*. New York: Stein and Day, 1972.

Armstrong, Louis. *Satchmo: My Life in New Orleans*. New York: Da Capo Press, 1954.

Balliett, Whitney. *American Musicians: 56 Portraits in Jazz*. New York: Oxford University Press, 1986.

Baraka, Amiri LeRoi Jones. *Blues People*. New York: William Morrow, 1963.

———. *Black Music*. New York: William Morrow, 1970.

Bechet, Sidney. *Treat It Gentle*. New York: Hill and Wang, 1960.

Berlin, Edward A. *King of Ragtime: Scott Joplin and His Era*. New York: Oxford University Press, 1994.

Berliner, Paul F. *Thinking in Jazz: The Infinite Art of Improvisation*. Chicago: University of Chicago Press, 1994.

Blesh, Rudi, and Janis, Harriet. *They All Played Ragtime*. New York: Oak Publications, 1966.

Cole, Bill. *Miles Davis: The Early Years*. New York: Da Capo Press, 1974.

Collier, James Lincoln. *The Making of Jazz: A Comprehensive History.* Boston: Houghton Mifflin, 1978.

———. *Louis Armstrong: An American Success Story.* New York: Collier, 1985.

Cook, Richard, and Morton, Brian. *The Penguin Guide to Jazz on CD, LP and Cassette.* London: Penguin, 1994.

Crow, Bill. *Jazz Anecdotes.* New York: Oxford University Press, 1990.

Dance, Stanley. *The World of Duke Ellington.* New York: Charles Scribner's Sons, 1970.

———. *The World of Count Basie.* New York: Charles Scribner's Sons, 1980.

Davis, Miles, with Quincy Troupe. *Miles: The Autobiography.* New York: Simon and Schuster, 1989.

Ellington, Edward Kennedy "Duke." *Music Is My Mistress..* New York: Doubleday, 1973.

Feather, Leonard. *The Book of Jazz.* revised and expanded. New York: Dell, 1957, 1965, 1976.

———. *The Encyclopedia of Jazz.* New York: Da Capo Press, 1957.

———. *The Encyclopedia of Jazz in the Sixties.* New York: Da Capo Press, 1967.

Friedwald, Will. *Jazz Singing.* New York: Collier, 1990, 1992.

Giddins, Gary. *Celebrating Bird: The Triumph of Charlie Parker.* New York: Beechtree Books, 1987.

———. *Satchmo.* New York: Dolphin/Doubleday, 1988.

Gillespie, Dizzy, with Al Fraser. *To Be or Not to Bop.* New York: Doubleday, 1979.

Giola, Ted. *The Imperfect Art: Reflections on Jazz and Modern Culture.* New York: Oxford University Press, 1988.

Gitler, Ira. *Jazz Masters of the Forties.* New York: Macmillan, 1966.

———. *Swing to Bop: An Oral History of the Transition of Jazz in the 1940's.* New York: Oxford University Press, 1985.

Goldberg, Joe. *Jazz Masters of the Fifties*. New York: Macmillan, 1965.

Hasse, John Edward. *Beyond Category: The Life and Genius of Duke Ellington*. New York: Simon and Schuster, 1993.

Hentoff, Nat. *Jazz Is*. New York: Limelight, 1976.

———. *The Jazz Life*. New York: Da Capo Press, 1961.

———. *Jazz Panorama*. New York: Collier, 1964.

Hobsbawm, Eric. *The Jazz Scene*. Revised and expanded. New York: Pantheon Books, 1992.

Hodier, Andre. *Jazz: Its Evolution and Essence*. New York: Grove Press, 1956.

Holiday, Billie, with William Dufty. *Lady Sings the Blues*. New York: Doubleday, 1956.

Keil, Charles. *Urban Blues*. Chicago: University of Chicago Press, 1968.

Kernfeld, Barry, ed. *The New Grove Dictionary of Jazz*. Revised and updated. New York: St. Martin's Press, 1988, 1994.

Kofsky, Frank. *Black Nationalism and the Revolution in Music*. New York: Pathfinder, 1970.

Lange, Art, and Nathaniel Mackey, eds. *Moment's Notice: Jazz in Poetry and Prose*. Minneapolis: Coffee House Press, 1993.

Larkin, Philip. *All That Jazz: A Record Diary, 1961–1971*. New York: Farrar, Straus & Giroux, 1985.

Lees, Gene. *Meet Me at Jim and Andy's*. New York: Oxford University Press, 1988.

———. *Jazz Lives: 100 Portraits in Jazz*. New York: Firefly, 1992.

Litweiler, John. *The Freedom Principle: Jazz after 1958*. New York: William Morrow, 1984.

———. *Ornette Coleman: A Harmolodic Life*. New York: William Morrow, 1992.

Lomax, Alan. *Mister Jelly Roll: The Fortunes of Jelly Roll Morton, New Orleans Creole and "Inventor of Jazz."* New York: Pantheon, 1950, 1978.

Marquis, Donald. *In Search of Buddy Bolden.* Baton Rouge: Louisiana State University Press, 1987.

Meltzer, David, ed. *Reading Jazz.* San Francisco: Mercury House, 1993.

Murray, Albert. *Stomping the Blues.* New York: McGraw-Hill, 1976.

O'Meally, Robert. *Lady Day: The Many Faces of Billie Holiday.* New York: Arcade, 1991.

Oliver, Paul. *Savanna Syncopators: African Retentions in the Blues.* New York: Stein and Day, 1970.

Porter, Lewis, ed. *The Lester Young Reader.* Washington, D.C.: Smithsonian Institution, 1991.

Reisner, Robert G. *Bird: The Legend of Charlie Parker.* New York: Citadel Press, 1962.

Russell, Ross. *Jazz Style in Kansas City and the Southwest.* Berkeley: University of California Press, 1971.

———. *Bird Lives! The High Life and Hard Times of Charlie Parker.* New York: Charterhouse, 1973.

Schuller, Gunther. *Early Jazz: Its Roots and Musical Development.* New York: Oxford University Press, 1968.

———. *The Swing Era: The Development of Jazz 1930–1945.* New York: Oxford University Press, 1989.

Shapiro, Nat, and Nat Hentoff. *Hear Me Talkin' to Ya.* New York: Holt, Rinehart and Winston, 1955.

Shaw, Arnold. *The Street That Never Slept: New York's Fabled 52nd Street.* New York: Coward McCann and Geoghegan, 1971.

———. *Honkers and Shouters: The Golden Years of Rhythm and Blues.* New York: Macmillan, 1978.

Sidran, Ben. *Black Talk.* New York: Da Capo Press, 1971.

Spellman, A. B. *Four Lives in the Bebop Business.* New York: Pantheon, 1966.

Stearns, Marshall W. *The Story of Jazz.* New York: Oxford University Press, 1956.

Tirro, Frank. *Jazz: A History.* revised and updated. New York: Norton, 1977, 1993.

Tucker, Mark, ed. *The Duke Ellington Reader*. New York: Oxford University Press, 1993.

Walton, Ortiz M. *Music: Black, White and Blue*. New York: William Morrow, 1972.

Williams, Martin. *The Jazz Tradition*. second revised edition. New York: Oxford University Press, 1993.

————. *Where's the Melody?: A Listener's Introduction to Jazz*. New York: Da Capo Press, 1966.

Wilmer, Valerie. *As Serious As Your Life*. London: Alison & Busby, 1977.

NOTE ON VIDEOS

Both "Satchmo: Louis Armstrong" (1988, Toby Byron Multiprises/CBS Music Video Enterprises, 87 minutes) and "Celebrating Bird: The Triumph of Charlie Parker". (1987, Toby Byron Multiprises, 59 minutes) are worthy introductions to their subjects.

ALSO RECOMMENDED

"The Sound of Jazz" (1990, Vintage Jazz Classics, Ltd., 58 minutes): A historic segment from a 1957 CBS-TV series, "The Seven Lively Arts," which features performances by Count Basie, Thelonious Monk, Red Allen and Billie Holiday.

"Art Blakey, The Jazz Messenger" (1988, Rhapsody Films, Inc.): a British-made documentary about the drummer-bandleader-mentor.

"The Universal Mind of Bill Evans" (45 minutes, Rhapsody Films, Inc.): The pianist discusses his life and work, with demonstrations.

"Thelonious Monk: Straight, No Chaser" (1989, Warner Home Video): The most revealing biography of an enigmatic composer.

RECOMMENDED LISTENING

What follows is not necessarily a "best album" list, although most of the albums listed include some of the greatest jazz ever recorded. What I've done, instead, is choose roughly twenty-five albums or boxed sets that offer easy, engrossing access to jazz music in all its variety.

With the advent of boxed compact-disc collections, more historically significant jazz music is available. But the cost may be high. In some instances where a boxed set is cited. along with the number of discs and, whenever possible, tape cassettes), I've included a single disc that's a more affordable alternative. You might want to check your local library.

Some important names and recordings will be missing. But many of them can be found on what is, by far, the best recorded introduction to jazz's first century: *The Smithsonian Collection of Classic Jazz*, which is now available in a boxed set of CDs, LPs, or cassettes, or in five separate CD volumes.

Louis Armstrong "Portrait of the Artist as a Young Man, 1923–1934" (Columbia/Legacy/Smithsonian Institution Press), 4 CDs. Alternative: "Louis Armstrong and Earl Hines, Vol. IV" (Columbia).

Art Ensemble of Chicago "Nice Guys" (ECM). One of the few records that show how much fun experimentation can be).

Count Basie "The Complete Decca Recordings" (MCA/GRP), 3 CDs, 3 cassettes. Alternative: "Count Basie 1938–39" (Classics).

Sidney Bechet "The Best of Sidney Bechet" (Blue Note).

Art Blakey and the Jazz Messengers "Paris, 1958" (RCA/Bluebird).

Betty Carter "Inside Betty Carter" (Capitol Jazz).

Ornette Coleman "Beauty Is a Rare Thing" (Rhino/Atlantic), 6 CDs. Alternative: "The Shape of Jazz to Come" (Atlantic).

John Coltrane "A John Coltrane Retrospective—The Impulse Years" (Impulse/GRP), 3 CDs. Alternative: "My Favorite Things" (Atlantic).

Miles Davis "Kind of Blue" (Columbia).

Duke Ellington "The Blanton-Webster Band" (Bluebird), 3 CDs. Alternative: ". . . And His Mother Called Him Bill" (Bluebird).

Bill Evans "Explorations" (Original Jazz Classics).

Dizzy Gillespie "The Complete RCA Recordings" (BMG Bluebird).

Coleman Hawkins "The Genius of Coleman Hawkins" (Verve).

Billie Holiday "The Quintessential Billie Holiday, Vols. 1–9" (Columbia), 9 CDs and tapes. (These don't come in a box. You can buy them separately and any one of them will have something that will move you deeply. I like the later volumes. Others prefer the middle three.)

Robert Johnson "The Complete Recordings" (Columbia), 2 CDs and tapes.

Scott Joplin "Piano Rags by Scott Joplin," Joshua Rifkin, piano (Nonesuch Elektra/Warner).

Charles Mingus "Thirteen Pictures: The Charles Mingus Anthology" (Rhino/Atlantic), 2 CDs.

Thelonious Monk "The Complete Blue Note Recordings" (Blue Note), 4 CDs. Alternative: "Thelonious Alone in San Francisco" (Original Jazz Classics).

Jelly Roll Morton "The Complete Jelly Roll Morton, 1926–1930" (RCA/Bluebird), 5 CDs. Alternative: "The Pearls" (Bluebird).

Charlie Parker "The Complete Dial Sessions, 1946–47" (Stash), 4 CDs. Alternative: "Sweedish Schnapps" (Verve).

Bud Powell "The Complete Blue Note and Roost Recordings" (Blue Note), 4 CDs. Alternative: "The Genius of Bud Powell" (Verve).

Sonny Rollins "Saxophone Colossus" (Original Jazz Classics).

Art Tatum "The Complete Pablo Solo Masterpieces" (Pablo), 7 CDs. Alternative: Any of the volumes, sold individually.

Cecil Taylor "Jazz Advance" (Blue Note).

Sarah Vaughan "Sarah Vaughan with Clifford Brown" (Emarcy).

Fats Waller "Turn on the Heat" (RCA/Bluebird), 2 CDs.

INDEX